Life After
BREAD

"Don't let this slender volume fool you! Packed with truths and a gimlet-eyed view of the path to diagnosis, Eydi Bauer's journey to the gluten-free life connects the dots with a woman's heart and a physician's wisdom."

> – Jax Peters Lowell, author of
> *The Gluten-Free Bible, Aganist the Grain,*
> and *No More Cupcakes & Tummy Aches*

❧

"Dr. Bauer's book is an answer to the prayers of thousands, the missing piece of the puzzle in their health or lack of it. Allergies and sensitivities are a common thread in severe health conditions. If the cause is celiac disease or wheat or gluten sensitivity, nothing will solve the problem until the gluten is totally removed from the diet. Well written and to the point, this book is a must for physicians and patients alike!"

> – Dr. John Brimhall, author of
> *Solving the Health Puzzle with the 6 Steps to Wellness*

Life After
BREAD

Get Off Gluten and
Reclaim Your Health

Dr. Eydi Bauer, D.C.

*A doctor's personal journey from sickness to health,
with information you need about celiac disease —
the silent epidemic.*

Cypress House

Life After Bread
Get off Gluten and Reclaim Your Health
Copyright ©2009 byDr. Eydi Bauer, D.C.

Cypress House
155 Cypress Street
Fort Bragg, CA 95437
(800) 773-7782
www.cypresshouse.com

Book and cover design: Michael Brechner / Cypress House

Cover illustration: Dana Blencowe

Library of Congress Cataloging-in-Publication Data
Bauer, Eydi.
    Life after bread : get off gluten and reclaim your health / Eydi Bauer.
        p. cm.
"A doctor's personal journey from sickness to health, with information you need about celiac disease-the silent epidemic."
    Includes bibliographical references and index.
    ISBN 978-1-879384-77-4 (pbk. : alk. paper)
    1. Gluten--Health aspects--Popular works. 2. Gluten-free diet--Popular works. 3. Celiac disease--Popular works. I. Title.
    RC862.C44B38 2009
            362.196'399--dc22   2008039008

Printed in Canada
2 4 6 8 9 7 5 3 1

Dedication

To all those who have suffered ailments without answers, have been labeled as hypochondriacs, or have been told, "It's all in your head." This book is for you.

Acknowledgments

I thank my Mom, Ginger Farry, and my Dad, Robert Bauer, for getting to know me better as a healthy woman and supporting me in creating this book. I thank John Gray for his inspiration and encouragement. Thanks to Emily and Medea for their help with editing. Thanks to Dana for her love and support, and to Tai for his sweetness and all the gluten-free pancakes!

Contents

INTRODUCTION XIII

CHAPTER 1: MY STORY 1

*In the Beginning ♦ The Long Road to Diagnosis ♦ Childless and
Thirty ♦ My World Fell Apart ♦ My Journey from Sickness to
Health ♦ Physician Heal Thyself*

CHAPTER 2: THE TRUTH AND CONSEQUENCES
OF GLUTEN 13

*Are We A Gluten-Eatin', Pill-Poppin' Society? ♦ The Vicious
Cycle: Are You Gluten Intolerant? ♦ A Glutton for Gluten ♦
Inflammation — It Gives You an "itis" ♦ Autoimmune Reactions
♦ Migrating Symptoms ♦ Low Carbs: The Right Start ♦ Some
Simple Truths ♦ The 12 Simple Truths*

CHAPTER 3: CELIAC DISEASE 25

*The Most Common Conditions ♦ Celiac Disease Defined ♦
Why Must We Wait So Long for the Healthcare Community
to Recognize this Very Common Condition? ♦ Classic Textbook
Celiac Disease ♦ Associated Conditions*

CHAPTER 4: GLUTEN INTOLERANCE
IN THE MODERN DAY 31

*The Modern-day Plague of Obesity ♦ Signs and Symptoms Can
Affect Any Part of the Body ♦ Gluten Intolerance – What Can it
Affect? ♦ The Confusion ♦ Autoimmune Disease – The War Within
♦ Are My Symptoms Food Related? ♦ Common Symptoms of
Gluten Intolerance ♦ Conditions Associated with Gluten Intolerance*

♦ Anemia ♦ Irritable Bowel Syndrome ♦ Diabetes ♦ Fibromyalgia ♦
Chronic Fatigue ♦ Psychological Conditions ♦ Skin Lesions ♦
Infertility ♦ Our Organs – What They Do and What Goes
Wrong – Getting Technical ♦ The Liver ♦ Pancreas ♦ Sugar Stress ♦
Small Intestine ♦ Adrenal Glands ♦ Thyroid Gland ♦ Ileocecal Valve
♦ Allergy vs. Intolerance

CHAPTER 5: THIS IS YOUR BRAIN ON GLUTEN. 49
Say No to All White Powders ♦ Addiction and Allergy
♦ Psychiatric Disorders, or "Am I Going Crazy?" ♦ Brain
Chemistry Imbalances — Look to the Gut ♦ Unstable Blood Sugar
Leads to Unstable Brain Chemistry

CHAPTER 6: HOW TO GET TESTED. 55
Who Should Be Tested? ♦ Teenagers ♦ Getting Tested – It Starts
at Home ♦ Stool Tests – Three Simple Steps ♦ How do you know
if a child is suffering from gluten intolerance? ♦ Getting Your Kids
Tested ♦ Blood Tests ♦ Medical Tests for Celiac Disease ♦ Celiac
Disease or Gluten Intolerance – Genetic Markers ♦ Why Test
Stool? ♦ Elimination Diet ♦ The Good News

CHAPTER 7: THE GLUTEN-FREE DIET. 65
To Eat or Not to Eat: The Gluten-Free Diet ♦ What Contains
Gluten and What Not to Eat? ♦ What Can I Eat? Safe Foods ♦
Additives – Are They Safe? ♦ Questionable Additives ♦ Multiple
Food Reactions ♦ Lactose Intolerance – the Cheese that Binds ♦
Alcohol – Can I Drink to That? ♦ Healing Starts in the Kitchen
♦ Eating Out – Be a Card-carrying Member ♦ Questions to Ask
at Restaurants ♦ Sample Card ♦ Single and Celiac ♦ Nutritional
Supplement Recommendations ♦ What to Avoid and Not Eat
♦ Accidental Exposure to Gluten ♦ Labeling Laws as of January
2006 ♦ Gluten-free Shopping List

Contents

CHAPTER 8: UNCOVERING THE HIDDEN EPIDEMIC ... 81

Hide and Go Seek a Celiac ◆ Case Studies ◆ The Dilemma
of the Medical Paradigm ◆ My Disease Became My Teacher

CHAPTER 9: GLUTEN-FREE RECIPES 93

MAIN COURSE RECIPES 94

Gluten-free Meatloaf or Turkey Loaf ◆ Stir-fried Vegetables
and Rice ◆ Salmon Roll Sushi ◆ Quinoa Salad with Asparagus ◆
Simple Lemon-Pepper Turkey ◆ Chicken Parmesan ◆ Gluten-free
Lasagna (can be made dairy free) ◆ Tofu Blend (the dairy-free
option) ◆ Gluten-free Homemade French Fries

DESSERTS 100

Gluten-free Piecrust ◆ Pumpkin or Squash Pie Filling ◆ Eydi's
Favorite Gluten-free, Dairy-free Chocolate Milk ◆ Chocolate
Cake

RESOURCES AND GLUTEN-FREE PRODUCTS 103

ABOUT THE AUTHOR 109

Introduction

In the United States, we spend twice as much on healthcare as any other country spends, yet we're generally in poorer health: 65 percent of Americans are overweight; millions are on antidepressants; and one in three women will get cancer. More than 12 million people suffer from diabetes, and the number is growing. We are becoming sicker because of what we eat, and common foods are often the source of our health imbalances. Every street corner offers us both the poison and a pharmaceutical remedy for what ails us. Each year, the pharmaceutical companies spend $4 billion on advertising to insure that they sell us their products. We need a paradigm shift.

When we buy a car, we're given an owner's manual that explains the workings of the vehicle and which type of fuel it runs on, gasoline or diesel. You wouldn't put diesel fuel in a gas-engine car because it would cause internal damage. Unfortunately, our bodies don't come with an owner's manual that outlines the right foods to eat to keep everything functioning properly. Usually, we begin by eating what's available to us and what tastes good. Quite commonly, we crave the very foods that we're allergic to or intolerant of. Feeling achy, fatigued, or emotionally on edge are warning signs that we're giving our bodies the wrong fuel. Too often, medical doctors will medicate before they educate people about their diet. Many of us ignore the signals of pain and discomfort our bodies give us, because we don't realize that common foods could cause so much distress. Taking drugs simply masks important warning signs — it's like unplugging a fire alarm without checking to see where the smoke is coming from.

Had someone told me twenty years ago that my health would progressively worsen if I didn't remove one specific ingredient from my diet, I might not have believed it. It would have seemed too simple. If I had been told to give up foods containing wheat and gluten, which would have meant eliminating baked goods, breads, pasta, and cookies, I might have chosen to ignore that invaluable advice. Now, after a long and difficult battle with celiac disease, a form of gluten intolerance, I wish I'd been given this information decades ago. They say that hindsight is 20/20. I hope that my story inspires you to get your diet on the right path to living a healthy life — before it's too late.

I'm not talking about a new fad diet, but about a change in consciousness.

I am a doctor of chiropractic and an applied kinesiologist specializing in food allergy and nutritional testing. In my years of practice as a holistic doctor, I have seen a multitude of patients who are suffering from unexplained symptoms. Many have come to me when other doctors have failed to find the underlying problem. After making the connection between a common food intolerance that is causing the decline in the health of a vast number of my patients, including my own health, I felt an urgency to write this book. My intention is to help people identify a highly common yet often misunderstood food intolerance.

Introduction

> *Gluten intolerance is a serious nutritional epidemic that is causing a vast array of health problems in America. It is largely unrecognized by the Western medical establishment.*

Gluten intolerance is a sleeping epidemic that's affecting millions. As a chiropractor, I work with patients experiencing pain and malfunction. Sometimes their pain is structural, resulting from a bone out of proper alignment. Often, their pain is chemical, resulting from internal inflammation. I am continually amazed at the vast number of patients suffering symptoms of pain and inflammation from gluten sensitivity. These people often seek out care for back and joint pain, stiffness, headache, fatigue, digestive distress, or depression. You may be one of the millions diagnosed with irritable bowel syndrome, arthritis, chronic fatigue, psoriasis, anxiety, or a psychological problem. With a strict gluten-free diet you could find dramatic relief. It's time to wake up and see that balancing your health is within your own control.

During my years in practice, I have encountered countless patients who complain of symptoms such as joint pain, headache, fatigue, depression, and bowel problems. I've found a majority of these people to be reacting to gluten, the protein in wheat, rye, and barley. Once they remove all gluten from their diets, their symptoms clear up and their health improves. Food allergies, gluten intolerance, and celiac disease are extremely common, very serious, and often overlooked as underlying causes of body chemistry imbalance. I have combined facts about gluten intolerance with what I've learned through my own personal battle with celiac disease, one manifestation of gluten intolerance, and I've included information from the myriad newly diagnosed patients in my office, and from expanding worldwide research.

Gluten foods are everywhere, and unless you are consciously avoiding them, you probably eat gluten every day. Most of us have never even experienced life gluten-free, or felt our bodies, even for a few days, without this common contaminant. We are constantly inundated by wheat-based foods that taste great. We gobble them down like addicts, resulting in the deterioration of our nervous systems. Many of us become accustomed to chronic discomfort because it's been with us for so long that we don't know what it feels like to be healthy.

Chronic symptoms may be common, but they are not normal. You can well imagine that if you drank alcohol many times each day or took mind-altering drugs on a daily basis, your perception of what is normal or real would be seriously skewed. What if you were to hit yourself in the head with a hammer every single day of your life? And then one day you decide to stop. That would be a good day. The healing could begin, and so could a whole new perspective on life. Unless you have deliberately gone 100 percent off of gluten grains and flours for at least thirty days, you may have never actually experienced your brain healthy.

There is a sustainable, permanent diet to achieve your ideal weight, be free from pain and inflammation, and balance your physical and mental state. Just read on.

CHAPTER 1

My Story

I am a thirty-eight-year-old doctor who suffered for twenty years from unexplained symptoms. I was a carbohydrate and sugar addict, and was unwell for many years. I didn't see the link between my diet and my nausea, fatigue, joint pain, and hormonal and emotional imbalances. For breakfast I would eat frosted Pop-Tarts, donuts, coffee cake, or bagels — no cooking required. Lunch was usually a stop at McDonald's, the local pizzeria, or a sandwich. I often ate cookies before and after a pasta dinner.

I grew up suffering frequent stomach problems, fatigue, irregular menstrual periods, and unexplained emotional distress. I knew that I was sensitive to sweets and bread, but, like many others, I was also addicted to them. My mother, a single mom, worked full time, so no one monitored my cookie, donut, and muffin intake. All I knew was carbohydrates, and all I experienced was discomfort. I often became dizzy when exercising, and strained my joints easily. I wondered what was wrong with me.

I studied diligently to become a holistic doctor, and my body became an experimental laboratory. As I got older I tried different diets. For a while I ate less wheat and flour, hoping that was enough to make a difference. I was wrong. It wasn't until a serious health crisis that I realized the extent of damage and suffering a body can endure due to gluten intolerance.

1

My health problems began when I was ten, and they became the impetus for me to study natural healing and alternative therapies. I graduated chiropractic college at twenty-five, and to date have had over twelve years of experience treating patients. At the age of thirty-four I was finally diagnosed correctly with a form of gluten intolerance called celiac disease (also known as celiac sprue, primary malabsorption syndrome, nontropical sprue.) Becoming gluten free has changed and saved my life. I now want to share my story and shed some light on this highly common but often overlooked condition.

In the Beginning…

I remember being ten years old and feeling sick for long periods. I had neither a frame of reference for what being well felt like, nor the words nor the medical education to articulate what was happening inside me. My mother would take me to the local medical doctor in our town. I'm pretty sure he had a drinking problem. Mom worked as a copywriter at Doubleday Publishing, and as a perk she had access to free books. Since money was scarce, she would trade the doctor books on bird identification, Beatles anthologies, and large picture books about Marilyn Monroe for my office visits. The doctor would take my temperature, look in my ears, and listen to my heart. Then he would announce, "There's nothing wrong with you, you're fine" and hand me a lollipop.

I knew that something wasn't right, that I was sick, and I told him so. I was nauseated, tired, dizzy, and my stomach and body hurt. "Growing pains" was his answer. Mom would drive me home saying, "There is nothing wrong with you, the doctor said so, and I'm running out of books to give him."

I would suck on the malt-sweetened syrup ball on a stick that the doctor had given me, my stomach continuing to hurt. I remember thinking that the doctor didn't get it. Most doctors don't.

As a teenager, I struggled with poor health. Outwardly, I appeared vibrant, energetic, and attractive. I was short and thin, with a bloated belly that I was always self-conscious about. I was active and popular, but felt sick and fatigued. I wrote stories for the school paper, was in the National Honor Society, won writing awards, and was on the varsity soccer team. But inside I knew that something was very wrong with me. I tried to express it, but usually just acted out. I remember doctors, nurses, school psychologists, and teachers labeled my symptoms as growing pains, hormone imbalances, and troubled teenager syndrome. I often wondered if all kids hurt the way I did. When I played soccer, I would repeatedly sprain my ankles while running. My knees and legs would often hurt or feel fatigued and weak. I would go five or six months without a menstrual period, and then bleed excessively for three or four weeks. I had constant stomachaches. I was always hungry and tired. I cried every day. I was told that I was just looking for attention and to cut it out. I became depressed. I ate the typical American teenage diet: pizza, bagels, sandwiches, muffins, and cookies, completely unaware that I was poisoning myself.

The Long Road to Diagnosis

I saw many medical doctors. Often, they would run blood tests. I remember waiting in anticipation for the results. It wasn't that I wanted something to be wrong with me, but that I knew something was. I recall one doctor entering the exam room with my chart. His eyes sank down in his glasses as he scanned my lab results. "Well, there's nothing wrong with you; your blood levels are within normal range. You are healthy, except for a mild anemia."

I swallowed in disbelief of this supposedly good news. "How can that be? I'm so fatigued that getting out of bed feels like climbing Everest. My joints ache like I've been beaten by an angry mob. Everything I eat makes my stomach ache. I haven't had a period in six months. Recently, I've had insomnia, and have been anxious and very depressed. This must be something."

The doctor seemed unfazed. He wrote me a prescription for anti-anxiety medication and a referral to a psychologist. He said, "Maybe it's in your head. Get some sleep." Then he hurried off to his next patient, who probably had similar symptoms and would get the same lame advice.

Over the years I went to general practitioners, gynecologists, and internists. No one could find anything wrong with me except for a case of anemia. Because of irregular and excessive menstrual bleeding, I was put on birth control pills at age fifteen. The pill made me sicker, causing severe headaches and vomiting. None of these highly educated medical professionals had a clue as to what was wrong with me, and the drugs they prescribed just made things worse. **No doctor ever questioned my diet.** I began to see that there was something wrong not just with me, but with the entire healthcare system if this was all it had to offer.

I decided to study alternative healing to get to the bottom of my own health struggles and to shift from the misguided medical model I had experienced. At age eighteen I left my home in New York and moved to California to study massage and acupressure at Heartwood Institute, a holistic school. Then I studied for four years at Life Chiropractic College West, where I specialized in applied kinesiology and clinical nutrition. I got married at the age of twenty-two, and graduated with a doctorate in chiropractic at the age of twenty-five.

There were times when my health seemed better. I experimented with different diets, continued to study nutrition, and took the best supplements. Since I seemed to have problems digesting cheese, I assumed — as many celiacs do before they're diagnosed — that I was lactose intolerant, and cut out dairy products. For a while I tried the Zone diet, from Dr. Barry Sears, which suggests cutting down on bad carbs, those with a high glycemic index such as breads, pastas, and desserts. I loved this diet, which helped me initially, and I felt that everyone could benefit from reducing high-glycemic carbohydrates. This diet is on the right track, but it doesn't specifically address gluten, a hidden source of distress in so many people. Following the Zone helped me feel better, but I never stayed well for long; I still was suffering a variety of symptoms. I read the *Merck Manual of Diagnosis and Therapy* cover to cover, and thought I had almost everything in the book, leading my husband to conclude that I was a hypochondriac.

I began my practice in northern California, and my schedule was full almost immediately. Dedicating myself to my patients, I had a successful practice within months. It was a thrill to be effecting a positive change in my patients. I worked at a rural nonprofit health clinic that offered everything from prenatal care to alternative therapies such as acupuncture and counseling. I was working hard, spending many hours treating patients, and I always felt fatigued. More often than not I'd come home with pain in all of my joints. I was successful in helping other people get well with hands-on therapy, but the cause of my own distress still eluded me.

At age twenty-six I ached the way I imagined an old woman would. I constantly felt run-down. I was plagued with stomachaches, a bloated belly, constipation, and irregular periods. Whenever I exercised or worked hard I would injure myself. I would wake up every morning with my back, neck, or shoulders aching. The pains would migrate around my body. Most of the time, I felt weak and depleted. I knew that many people were tired and fatigued, but I believed that just because it was common didn't mean it was normal.

Based on my many symptoms I believed that I had an auto-immune disease, and the medical doctor in my rural town concurred. It seemed to be of unknown origin. I had a positive lab test called ANA (anti-nuclear antibody), which tests for antibodies against your own cells, and is a nonspecific autoimmune finding. I researched the autoimmune conditions lupus, scleroderma, rheumatoid arthritis, psoriatic arthritis, and celiac sprue. Since I'd been tested for some of these diseases and they had been ruled out, I questioned my doctor about celiac. There wasn't much information about it in the medical books. What they did say was: "a disease of childhood… with weight loss, diarrhea, and weakness." Although I was of slight stature, I wasn't losing weight or experiencing diarrhea, but I did have irritable bowel symptoms and constipation issues.

The doctor suggested that I stop eating wheat for a while to see if I'd feel any better. He did no tests, and there was no discussion to educate me about the extent of the gluten-free diet. I received no warnings of the hidden sources of gluten such as meats marinated in soy sauce (which contains wheat), flour used as a thickener in soups, food starch, barley malt in nutrition bars, even French fries sharing the same fryer oil as breaded fried foods. Gluten was in everything. I tried a wheat-free diet for a while, since the standard test for celiac disease at that time was an intestinal biopsy, which seemed too invasive.

Sometimes I felt better, and I tried to stay off wheat, but I ate cookies or a slice of pizza here and there. I switched to spelt bread, which is wheat free but not gluten free. I didn't have the whole picture, only parts of the puzzle. The diet was strict and I wasn't, so my symptoms returned. I didn't want to believe that eating wheat could make me so sick. It seemed to me that if wheat was responsible for so much suffering, it would be more recognized by the medical community. Wouldn't there be a warning label on every package of cupcakes like the warning on alcohol and cigarettes? I figured something else must be causing my problems, since I had tried the diet by going off wheat, as the doctor vaguely recommended. So I went back on wheat and, continuing my search for an explanation, moved on to the next specialist. I didn't know that I had been on the right track, but that *any* amount of gluten, even one bite, would initiate an immune reaction. There's simply no cheating, because you only cheat yourself. Often I was comforted by carbohydrates and baked goods, and I slowly slid back into eating those foods, unaware that the worst was yet to come. It would be seven more years before I received a confirmed diagnosis.

Childless and Thirty

Like most women, I wanted to have a baby. Throughout my marriage, during my late twenties and early thirties, I had tried to get pregnant, but suffered from infertility alternating with miscarriages. My periods came erratically and then overstayed their welcome like an oblivious houseguest. I would bleed for weeks at a time and then not for many months. By age thirty, I had had three miscarriages, and became successively weaker with each one. I continued my practice, seeing nearly a hundred patients a week, but I became chronically fatigued. Arriving home after treating patients, I would go straight to bed. My husband tried to be supportive; he cooked for me and helped take care of the house. At that point nearly everything I ate made my stomach ache and bloat or nauseated me. I was hypoglycemic and hungry all the time. I was developing a nervous tremor, so I decided to see another specialist. I remember making a three-hour drive to San Francisco to visit an endocrinologist. I trembled with the vibration of the car, shaking so much that I thought I was becoming diabetic. As I sat in the doctor's office and explained my distress, I burst into tears. The doctor ran blood tests. Her findings indicated it was not diabetes (at least not yet). She told me to eat more protein and less sugar (good advice, but missing the mark.) She also referred me to a psychologist. My husband was beginning to believe the popular prejudice that it was all in my head.

During this uncomfortable journey, a mental rant accompanied the autoimmune physical ailments, almost like the sound track to a movie. When my body felt a crescendo of symptoms — exhaustion, nausea, bloating, nervousness, weakness, and flu-like conditions — the background chatter and noise in my mind would increase in intensity as well.

> *For years, I experienced what I called "oxygen hunger." It was a combination of dizziness and the inability to breathe fully. Often, when I stood up quickly I felt that I would fall over. This was due to anemia and hypoxia. A lack of absorption of B12 results in anemia and a decreased ability to carry oxygen to the cells. I would gobble up air in the same manner as I inhaled food, to no avail. I could not satiate the hunger.*

As a compassionate practitioner, I continued treating patients even when I wasn't feeling well. I cared deeply about my patients' pain and suffering because I could empathize with them. I felt dedicated to alleviating pain wherever I could. My intuition and palpation skills were becoming keen. Many of my patients were improving under my care, and this was the one thing in my life that was successful, so I worked myself to utter exhaustion. All my energy went into facilitating improvement in patients, and most of them were getting better. I didn't understand why my own health was not improving.

When I Turned Thirty-two My World Fell Apart

By that time my health was gone and my mind was going with it. I could no longer function. I couldn't digest food without bloating or pain, so I avoided eating. Plagued with insomnia, I was up most nights, my heart and mind racing in tormented darkness. It was hard to have a coherent thought, and there was no relief in sight. I was a very intelligent, highly educated, successful young woman, and I was watching my mind deteriorate. In rare moments of lucidity, I observed my condition and thought *this must be what autoimmune disease and mental illness feels like.*

I stopped seeing patients full-time and became a full-time patient. I visited countless doctors and specialists; they all gave me different drugs that didn't help. I would lie in bed feeling exhausted, all of my joints hurting. A low-grade sore throat had been with me for months; it felt like I was always fighting an infection. I was nauseated, depressed, and nervous, and had begun losing weight. I went for HIV and hepatitis tests, both negative. A second endocrinologist suspected that I had a brain tumor and ordered an MRI of my pituitary gland. The brain scan was normal. I was put on anti-depressant and anti-seizure medications to help me sleep. I now feared that a mental illness might be consuming me. Then my husband of twelve years left me. It felt like the end of my life. And it was the end — of *that* life. Thank God.

My Journey from Sickness to Health

I was thirty-four years old and looked like a young girl. Five feet one inch tall and weighing ninety-five pounds, I appeared petite and youthful, but I felt like a fragile old woman. I was fighting a losing battle with an invisible enemy inside me. It was hard to mend, and I was weary in every way. Cooking seemed impossible, so I ate bread for breakfast and pasta for dinner. I continued seeking help but was becoming despondent. For two years, I had been on a slew of medications from various medical doctors. The drugs had decreased my sensitivity to all the symptoms. Weekly acupuncture and chiropractic treatments helped me function day to day. In weary hope of an explanation, I continued to search.

In 2004 I was blessed with an answer from a healthcare practitioner. I filled out a new patient medical history form for what was probably the hundredth time. Under STATE YOUR COMPLAINTS I listed chronic fatigue, joint pain, weakness, depression, menstrual problems, infertility, miscarriages, insomnia, stomachaches, bloating, and lactose intolerance. I listed the digestive problems last because they weren't my primary symptoms.

In one hour this doctor explained that *all* of my symptoms could be arising from celiac disease, one form of gluten intolerance. Stool tests confirmed the diagnosis. A lifetime of suffering and it had been this all along. All of my seemingly unrelated health problems finally made sense. Celiac disease had not presented itself as the textbooks describe it. I thought about the three babies I had lost — miscarriage is common with undiagnosed celiac disease. I had experienced malnourishment and toxicity to the brain that made me feel like I was losing my mind. I felt very mixed emotions at first. *How could so many doctors have overlooked this for so long? If I change my diet and really eliminate all gluten, will I get better? This diet is so strict, can I do it? Is this just one more thing I'll have to endure without any lasting results?*

With positive lab tests and a confirmed diagnosis in hand, I finally knew what I had to do.

Physician Heal Thyself

Celiac disease is not a terminal diagnosis, but it requires lifelong dietary change. It may sound simple, but it was far from easy. Could I really never eat pizza or chocolate cake again? How could life be so unfair?

Once your illness is identified, you are the one who has to take the steps to heal yourself every day, choosing gluten-free foods. With the guidance of a good healthcare professional, you become your own doctor. After all, no one knows how your body feels and functions better than you do. By adhering to a strict, lifelong gluten-free diet and proper nutrition you will regain your health. There's no medication, no surgery, no ongoing treatment. It's all about *you* making the lifestyle changes at home and educating the restaurants and grocery stores that you frequent so you can have gluten-free alternatives.

Within weeks of removing *all* gluten from my diet I began waking up in a body that was free of pain. Calmness that I had never experienced before washed over me. My mind was filled with blissfully unfamiliar peace and quiet. My lifelong bowel problems cleared almost immediately, and my bloated belly finally flattened. For years I had had persistent pain and swelling in my lower right abdomen, in the area of the ileocecal valve, and it too released. My energy level increased and I found that I had the strength to exercise. It was the miracle I had been praying for. I shed my first tears of joy. Cut free from shackles, I got my life back at thirty-four. I am now thirty-eight years old, have been gluten free for four years, and am healthier and happier than I've ever been. I started having profound realizations. All of my seemingly unrelated symptoms were completely diet induced, caused by the foods I put in my body. I became proactive in recovery from celiac disease, and with a new road map, I've learned how to eat to feel well. I'd like to share with all of you what else I've learned.

CHAPTER 2

The Truth and Consequences of Gluten

Gluten is the protein portion in wheat, rye, and barley grains. It is the substance that makes flour sticky in breads, bagels, rolls, pasta, cookies, and cakes. Gluten breaks down to a fraction called *gliadin*, and no one digests gliadin completely.

Are We A Gluten-Eatin', Pill-Poppin' Society?

Many Americans have grown accustomed to eating foods that are ready fast, and then grabbing a quick cure for the resulting ailments. We poison ourselves with processed foods and then pop pills to feel better. For example, if you buy boxed cereal like frosted Wheaties or Cheerios for breakfast, and need to have a 250-count bottle of Ibuprofen on hand, there may be a connection. On the same aisle in nearly every market, we are offered both endless choices of these offending gluten foods and the corresponding drug remedies. This product placement could come in handy when we need an electric wheelchair to get us into the store to buy more boxed cereals and over-the-counter painkillers.

Too many people are fatigued, have achy joints, headaches, muscle weakness, and abdominal distress. I see it in my office every day. In addition, millions are mentally and emotionally stressed, labeled with depression or anxiety or told it's something "in your head." More antidepressant medication is prescribed in the US than any other type of drug. It is estimated that 25 percent of Americans suffer from mental disorders ranging from depression to bipolar disorder. If you are experiencing vague symptoms and ignoring them or taking drugs to feel better you're probably developing a chronic condition. Listen to your body — it's trying to tell you something. It makes sense to get your body back to balanced, healthy function before disease sets in and an arsenal of medication is prescribed.

Dr. Rodney Ford is a pediatric gastroenterologist who runs a busy clinic in New Zealand, specializing in food allergies. In his book, *Full of It: The Shocking Truth About Gluten*, Dr. Ford says:

> The shocking truth about gluten is that it is a food that is causing tremendous damage — but unrecognised. Gluten grains have become our staple diet. The quantity of gluten in our food has been steadily increasing. And official Health Policies endorse gluten grains as the foundation of our food pyramid.

We have been awash in a sea of misinformation. The food pyramid tells us to eat six to eight servings of breads and cereals per day. This is way off base, unless you want to create a huge, achy, sick body. Bottom line: if you eat like the pyramid, you'll look like a pyramid.

The Vicious Cycle:
Are You Gluten Intolerant?

Ask yourself these questions: Do you feel tired most of the time? Do you have joint pain or numbness? Is it difficult for you to exercise without pain? Do you have reccurring injuries? Does your stomach ache or bloat after meals? Do you suffer depression, anxiety, mental imbalances, or mood swings? Are you infertile, or have you had recurring miscarriages? Do you sometimes hurt all over? Do you have problems with your weight? Do you wonder what's wrong with you? Have you been told that it's all in your head?

If you answered yes to more than one question, then it's time to consider the foods you eat as a source of your distress. Look at your diet for the past several days. Have you eaten breads, cereals, bagels, muffins, pizza, pasta, cookies, or fried breaded foods? Unless you're going out of your way to avoid them, gluten foods are being offered to you at every meal. Most of what people consume every day contains wheat and gluten.

Without knowing it you may be poisoning yourself every time you eat. Gluten intolerance is often the silent root cause underlying many other illnesses. Millions of Americans are being labeled with a variety of conditions that are actually reactions to gluten.

Current worldwide research is available about gluten-related health problems. Just Google "gluten intolerance" to get a crash course online. Read some of the millions of articles and you'll know more than most medical doctors about this topic.

Our heavily wheat-based diets are a major cause of distress and disease, yet most Americans are oblivious, eating crackers and cookies in front of the TV while commercials suggest that they ask their doctor about some happy pill to make all their symptoms go away (side effects may include dry mouth, vomiting, stroke, or heart failure.) Why don't we see TV commercials about these food intolerances? Public service announcements should inform us about these toxic foods, which are as detrimental to our health as tobacco smoking.

I'm all for a new ad campaign: GOT GLUTEN? GOT PAIN?

A Glutton for Gluten

Gluten is a big part of the modern-day life. At every store, restaurant, bakery, and rest stop in America, we are being served this culprit. Most foods that we grab on the go — bagels, sandwiches, pizza, and almost any fast food — contain gluten. In our hurried, busy lives, we lose sight of how to cook and how to feed ourselves properly. We consider a bagel or a bowl of cereal a meal. Fast foods may be a quick and easy choice, but they come at the high cost of our physical and emotional well-being. When we eat wheat or flour products, the gluten protein is not broken down completely. **No one digests gluten proteins completely**. These undigested protein particles stay in our systems and lead to a condition called inflammation, which is the cause of most pain and disease.

Inflammation — It Gives You an "itis"

Any condition ending in "itis" means inflammation — colitis, tendinitis, bursitis, gastritis, arthritis, or myofascitis. Inflammation is usually noted by chronic pain, swelling, heat, or loss of function in an area. When inflammation affects the joints it is called arthritis; in the tendons, it's tendinitis, and when it affects the digestive system it's called colitis or gastritis, and so on.

The cover of *Time* magazine (Feb. 2004) named inflammation "The Secret Killer." Most of the time, inflammation is a lifesaver;

it enables our bodies to defend against invading material or pathogens. When inflammation becomes chronic, however, the body turns on itself, allowing inflammation to lead to a wide variety of diseases. Remember: Gluten proteins don't break down completely in the digestive tract, and these undigested proteins are the source of inflammation in many people. In certain people, perhaps 30 percent of the population, the immune system reacts to gluten proteins as if an infection were present, by "walling them off." Most people consume gluten at every meal, which means there's an ongoing inflammatory condition. We have a choice: we can take anti-inflammatory drugs, or we can eliminate the gluten foods that cause disease.

All pain is caused by inflammation. The primary focus of medicine since the beginning of time has been the search for compounds that reduce pain. Yet your doctor may be at a complete loss to explain what inflammation is and how it triggers pain in the body.

— Dr. Barry Sears
The Anti-Inflammation Zone

Autoimmune Reactions

Our immune system is designed to protect us by making white blood cells to attack and engulf bacteria and other harmful substances. An autoimmune reaction occurs when the immune system turns on itself, attacking the body's own tissues. When there is an accumulation of undigested food proteins in the body, the immune system treats these undigested particles as foreign material, similar to an infection that must be destroyed. Your immune system makes antibodies, which attack foreign proteins. This process leads to inflammation, and this can affect any part of your body. If you have an autoimmune reaction to gluten, after eating pizza you may experience bloating, constipation, fatigue, brain fog, shoulder pain, headache, or generalized achiness. These symptoms may take a few hours to appear, or may occur a few days after the exposure. Many diseases are now found to be autoimmune in nature, such as diabetes, rheumatoid arthritis, Crohn's disease, psoriasis, and other skin diseases. It may take years to develop a diagnosable disease, or you may experience immediate discomfort. Autoimmune diseases are becoming more and more prevalent. Women are three times more likely than men to develop an autoimmune disease.

Migrating Symptoms

One interesting thing about patients with gluten intolerance is that they often complain of symptoms that vary and shift from place to place in the body. Commonly, they have a wide variety of ailments. For example, one week a person may experience neck pain that travels into the right shoulder, and the next week have lower-back pain, knee pain, or generalized achy joints. Migrating headaches, digestive distress, weakness, and fatigue may be part of the picture. This is because inflammation and autoimmune reactions will affect many different organs. These may be associated with ongoing depression, mood swings, and anxiety. Many people live with discomfort and remain undiagnosed until they develop more chronic health problems or associated autoimmune disease. Another thing to note is that the absence of symptoms doesn't mean that there's no damage from a given food. In fact, a large percentage of people who are not experiencing symptoms will eventually develop illnesses from ingesting gluten.

Millions of people suffer from a variety of problems arising from undiagnosed gluten intolerance. Long-term outcomes can include heart disease, diabetes, arthritis, osteoporosis, mental illness, and autoimmune diseases such as lupus, thyroiditis, and rheumatoid arthritis, all of which may be gluten induced. If you are one of these people, or know someone struggling with an ongoing health problem, a gluten-free diet may save your life. You may be aboard the *Titanic*, and these offending grains and flours are the iceberg. It makes sense to tailor your diet the way you would tailor your clothes to fit your body. It's time to get off of the foods that are eroding your health and well-being.

Low Carbs: The Right Start

Why Low-Carb Diets Are on the Right Track … but Not Enough

Low-carb diets are essentially low-gluten diets. Popular diet plans such as Atkins, The Zone, and the South Beach Diet all recommend eating few or no carbohydrates. They share warnings about the danger of bad carbs. Many people do very well on these diets: they lose weight, have more energy, and feel better. If you're already doing this, then you're more than halfway there. The missing piece, the key to regaining and sustaining health, is to remove all gluten-containing carbohydrates from your diet.

Enter The Zone by Dr. Barry Sears is a very popular book about restricting carbohydrates in our diets. Dr. Sears's research and nutrition plan focus on eliminating the "bad carbs" to balance our blood sugar and insulin, prevent inflammation and disease, and enhance mental clarity by staying in "the Zone." He suggests turning our diets back to primitive times, eating proteins such as meat and other animal products, vegetables, beans, and rice. According to Sears, the diet of Paleolithic humans featured virtually no grains or starches. This is definitely the right track. Our genetic make-up was not to eat wheat, especially wheat processed to come neatly packaged in colorful cereal and pasta boxes. Only in the last 10,000 years has wheat entered our diet. The human digestive tract evolved over 100,000 years without wheat.

Getting back to the basics of whole foods and saying no to processed foods (most of the foods that are sold in boxes or plastic bags) is certainly the way to good health. There have been many books about low-carb diets. All of these programs are headed in the right direction, but they're still missing a big piece of the puzzle: total elimination of wheat and other carbohydrates that contain gluten. If you're experimenting with one of those diets, you're on your way to being gluten free. Now, follow the gluten-free diet (see chapter 7) and go 100 percent off of gluten. You'll be amazed at how much better your mind and body will feel when you try it. The answer to so many people's suffering is to eliminate *all* wheat and other gluten grains.

Some Simple Truths

As a holistic doctor, I see a great deal of food-intolerant sickness. I have found that almost all of the patients I treat for chronic pain have gluten sensitivities. When put on a gluten-free diet, these patients reported improvement or complete resolve of back pain, carpal tunnel syndrome, headaches, bloating, fatigue, depression, anxiety, numbness, stomach cramping, constipation, and itchy skin conditions, to name just a few. This led me to discover...

The 12 Simple Truths

1. If you have any chronic health problem you may be gluten intolerant. Symptoms of joint pain and aches, fatigue, digestive problems, bloating, numbness, infertility, weight issues, or any autoimmune disease are often resolved by a gluten-free diet.

2. The more carbohydrates that you eat, the worse you'll feel. I don't recommend trying it, but have you ever noticed how lethargic you become after eating a bowl of pasta, some bread, and then cake for dessert? It's probable that deeper damage is being done.

3. Mental and emotional distress can be directly caused by poor eating habits. Depression, anxiety, mood swings, panic attacks, and even mental illness can be signs of long-standing gluten intolerance. In some people, eating gluten grains can cause a lack of absorption of nutrients due to damage to the intestines and other organs. When this happens, one can become malnourished. If certain nutrients aren't absorbed properly, a person cannot make serotonin, the neurotransmitter that the brain needs to feel happy and content. Nutritional deficiencies lead to imbalances in brain chemistry. (This is why so many Americans are on Prozac and other mood-altering drugs. Remember: more anti-depressant medications are prescribed in the US than any other drug.)

4. Gluten sensitivity is a neurological disease. Any organ or system in the body supplied by the brain and the nerves can be damaged by gluten sensitivity. This means that *all* systems can be affected — digestive, nervous, reproductive, musculoskeletal, as well as your psychological functioning.

5. Most people benefit from a low-carbohydrate, gluten-free diet. Many popular diets have already begun the trend toward decreasing carbohydrates. Low-carb diets are essentially low-gluten diets. To perfect this, avoid the dangerous carbohydrates by going 100 percent gluten free. Eat only the safe carbs such as rice, corn, millet, and quinoa (see the section on grains in chapter 7).

6. Recent studies have estimated that up to 40 percent (nearly half) of our population has antibodies against gluten and will suffer a wide range of symptoms. Celiac disease is only one manifestation of gluten intolerance, which is now being called the most common and the most under-diagnosed autoimmune disease of our time.

7. If you have celiac disease, you are by definition gluten intolerant. It means that your immune system damages your small intestines whenever you ingest gluten molecules. This is an autoimmune disease, and recovery is possible on a proper gluten-free diet.

8. Gluten intolerance is not just for celiacs anymore. Detrimental effects of gluten are not limited to the small intestine. Many people with gluten sensitivities develop problems with the pancreas, liver, bones, joints, skin, heart, spleen, kidney, thyroid, reproductive organs, or mental function. Undigested gluten particles can damage *any* part of the body.

9. Eliminating gluten from your diet can prevent diabetes, thyroid conditions, mental disorders, osteoporosis, celiac disease, and other autoimmune diseases. The connection between gluten sensitivity and the development of chronic illnesses has been well documented.

10. There has never been a better time to go gluten free. New gluten-free products are popping up everywhere, from Pamela's Products and baked goods to Whole Foods Market Gluten-Free Bakery selections of rice and almond breads, cookies, and pies. Make informed decisions when you shop and cook. Do some reading at the grocery store.

11. Your intuition is your best friend. If you suspect that something isn't right with your health, trust that feeling, examine what you eat, and pay attention to how your body responds. You and only you are responsible for what goes in your mouth every day. You have the power to change your diet and re-balance your life.

12. Only two aisles in the grocery store offer you nutritious foods: the meat, poultry, and fish aisle and the produce aisle (fruits and vegetables). Make a pit stop for rice, quinoa, dairy, and eggs. Most of the remaining aisles are filled with colorfully boxed junk.

CHAPTER 3

Celiác Disease

We are dealing with the most under-diagnosed and misdiagnosed autoimmune illness of our time. Most celiacs suffer for an average of eleven years before a proper diagnosis is made. Only a small percentage of people with celiac disease fit the classic picture of symptoms. Gluten-intolerant patients are often missed altogether, and go on to develop other diseases.

This section provides additional medical and scientific information.

The Most Common Conditions
Before a Diagnosis of Celiac Disease

1. Anemia

2. Irritable bowel syndrome

3. Psychological stress – nerves or imagination

4. Diabetes

5. Spastic colon/diarrhea

6. Ulcers

7. Allergies

8. Chronic fatigue syndrome

9. Gastroenteritis/colitis

8. Fibromyalgia

9. Gastric reflux

10. Lactose intolerance

11. Gall bladder disease

12. Thyroid disease

Celiac Disease Defined

Celiac disease is an autoimmune reaction to gluten, the protein found in wheat, rye and barley. In celiac disease the immune system overreacts to gluten and attacks itself. When wheat or gluten grains are ingested and reach the small intestine, the immune system views them as an invader and attacks the villi lining the intestines. It's like hosting a civil war in the body. This is a multi-system disease; that is, it affects more than just the digestive organs.

Celiac disease is the most common and the most under-diagnosed autoimmune condition in the United States. It is also hereditary, meaning it runs in families. An excellent reference book is *Celiac Disease: A Hidden Epidemic* by Dr. Peter Green of Columbia University. Dr. Green's book should be required reading in medical schools.

Celiac disease has been called the "great pretender" because it mimics so many other conditions. This leaves people chasing symptoms and seeing countless specialists in search of answers. Some people have the classic digestive problems (bloating, stomach pain, cramps, constipation, or diarrhea). Others may have no digestive complaints, and often remain undiagnosed until another gluten-related illness is found, such as diabetes, autoimmune thyroiditis, osteoporosis, inflammatory bowel disease, liver dysfunction, skin disease, or mental illness. All of these can be long-term outcomes of underlying celiac disease or gluten intolerance.

It is possible to be celiac, or gluten intolerant, and have no digestive complaints. Instead, symptoms may manifest as fatigue, back and muscle pain, or easily strained and inflamed joints. Many people suffer for years, seeking help from healthcare professionals for a variety of problems without anyone identifying food as the source of their ailments. It is also common for people to experience psychological stress as their main complaint—irritability, emotional instability, or depression. On average, people suffer over ten years before receiving a proper diagnosis, consulting countless doctors and receiving faulty diagnoses and dead-end treatments until they discover the cause of their distress. By that time, more damage may have occurred.

Why Must We Wait So Long for the Healthcare Community to Recognize this Very Common Condition?

One reason is that celiac disease mimics so many other disorders and affects multiple systems in the body. It is difficult to have a list of symptoms to fit a profile of celiac disease. Secondly, doctors are taught in medical school that celiac disease affects 1 in 4,000 people, when current research has found it affects 1 in 100. This is a huge difference. Gluten sensitivities are even more common: some sources report 1 person in 3 is gluten intolerant. These conditions may not be on the medical doctors' radar, but they should be — they are one of the primary reasons why people get sick in this country. A recent article in *JAMA* reported that as many as one in thirty-three children and adolescents were found to have celiac disease.

Today's medical school curriculum lacks nutrition classes. According to Harvey Ross, M.D., in *Hypoglycemia: The Classic Healthcare Handbook*, it is scandalous that the average physician received such a lack of information and education on nutrition.

A third reason diagnosis is often delayed is that until recently there was no easy way to screen for these conditions. An intestinal biopsy used to be required to test for celiac disease. This invasive procedure required going to the hospital, and it was expensive. Now there are simple lab tests for gluten allergy, gluten intolerance, and celiac disease, all the reactions to gluten (see chapter 6 – How To Get Tested).

Finally, pharmaceutical companies are the ones who fund research. There has been little funding given to studying celiac disease and gluten intolerance. The powerful influence of drug companies has led researchers away from studying how diet affects many conditions. After all, the pharmaceutical industry is primarily interested in developing and profiting from new drugs. If you have celiac disease or a gluten-related illness, the treatment is 100 percent dietary. No drugs are required. The only place you'll need to spend your money and your time (reading labels) is at the grocery or health-food store. There's no waiting on long lines at the pharmacy.

Classic Textbook Celiac Disease

Once called "emaciating, incapacitating syndrome," textbook celiac disease is described as wasting away, with weight loss due to the malabsorption, diarrhea or runny stools, and a distended belly. There is fatigue and muscle weakness from the loss of nutrients, which can cause patients to present with numbness in the hands and feet, osteoporosis, depression, and irritability. Unfortunately, despite the telltale symptoms, these people are often misdiagnosed.

Associated Conditions

There are many associated conditions that arise when celiac disease has gone undetected. Neuropathy (nerve pain or numbness) of unknown origin is common in celiac patients. Bone loss, osteoporosis, arthritis, and joint problems are often-seen side effects of untreated celiac disease. A skin condition known as dermatitis herpetiformis, also called celiac of the skin, is a painful, intensely itchy rash of tiny red bumps or blisters often mistaken for eczema or psoriasis. Autoimmune thyroid disease, diabetes, liver or kidney disease, colitis, irritable bowel syndrome, chronic fatigue syndrome, and anemia are disorders that may occur because celiac disease has been overlooked. Mental disorders such as depression, anxiety, panic attacks, mood swings, manic/bipolar, or seizures can be the effects of celiac disease on the brain.

Dr. Rodney Ford, a pediatric gastroenterologist and allergist in New Zealand, has been studying the effects of gluten on patients for more than a decade. In his article "Gluten Causes Brain Disease" Dr. Ford states:

> I have been increasingly concerned by the large number of my patients who are affected by gluten. I was perplexed by their wide-ranging symptoms. The puzzle was to explain how gluten could cause so much ill health to so many people in so many different ways, including celiac disease.

In his studies, Dr. Ford concluded that gluten was similar to a neurotoxin; stating that "gluten was gradually damaging the brain and the nerves of susceptible people." Dr. Ford talks about celiac disease as being just one result of that damage. Instead of taking the center of the research stage it should be viewed as just one of many gluten mediated illnesses.

CHAPTER 4

Gluten Intolerance
in the Modern Day

We now know that millions of people are affected by gluten-related illnesses that are not yet represented in textbooks.

The Modern-day Plague of Obesity

You can be overweight and have celiac disease or gluten intolerance. In fact, weight gain and obesity are common results of gluten intolerance. Due to the damage of the lining of the small intestine, the body becomes unable to absorb nutrients, so when you eat, you don't get nourished. It literally feels like you're starving. Sufferers feel hungry despite having consumed enough calories, because they have vitamin and mineral deficiencies that can cause food cravings. The need for nutrients drives the individual to eat excess calories because he or she doesn't feel satiated. Continued consumption of gluten foods (bread, pasta, cookies, muffins, beer, etc.) will interfere with further nutrient absorption and create a vicious cycle of overeating to compensate. There may also be sugar cravings, or the patient may have hypoglycemia (low blood sugar). Recurrent episodes of hypoglycemia warrant a test for celiac disease/gluten intolerance.

31

People with gluten intolerance are now seen with weight gain, bloating, gas, and a tendency toward constipation. Inflammation in the gut can lead to joint pain, achiness, weakness, and fatigue. The most neglected group of undiagnosed celiac patients is those who are overweight. These patients need help, and their doctors are missing it. Studies show that 40 percent of celiac disease patients are overweight at diagnosis, and the number maybe higher. Obesity, diabetes, heart disease, thyroid problems, osteoporosis, and cancer can be long-term outcomes of untreated celiac disease or gluten intolerance.

Signs and Symptoms Can Affect Any Part of the Body

Gluten intolerance that causes damage to the small intestine is defined as celiac disease; however, other organs and systems can be harmed by gluten sensitivity.

The following is a chart that outlines all the possible areas affected and the outcomes.

Gluten Intolerance – What Can it Affect?

Areas Affected	Symptoms	Potential Outcomes
Small Intestine	Bloating, gas, stomach pain Cramping, diarrhea, constipation	Damaged villi, malabsorption Celiac disease, IBS
Muscle and bones	Joint pain, weakness Inability to exercise	Chronic sprains, torn ligaments Degenerative arthritis, Osteoporosis
Thyroid	Weight gain or weight loss Chronic fatigue	Low or high thyroid (Hashimoto's) Thyroiditis
Pancreas	Low blood sugar, indigestion Bloating, reflux, heartburn	Hypoglycemia, diabetes Lactose Intolerance
Liver	Anger, right-shoulder pain Nausea, backaches	Cirrhosis, liver disease, fatty liver
Ovaries	Irregular periods, cramping Heavy bleeding	Infertility, endometriosis Amenorrhea, miscarriages
Nervous System	Numbness, weakness, tingling	Neuropathies, seizures
Brain (mental)	Depression, anxiety, nervous Mood swings, temper tantrums	Schizophrenia, bipolar ADD, Mental Illness, Dementia

The Confusion

Here is the confusing part of the diagnostic process: You can be gaining weight or losing weight. You can have constipation or diarrhea. You can have none of the above and just exhibit mental instability and emotional problems from loss of nutrients, neurological damage, and autoimmune reactions. You can have inflammation that appears as arthritis and joint pain with migrating numbness. You can feel exhausted and have weakness similar to having flu. This is a medical dilemma. These can all be related to gluten intolerance and be labeled as a host of other illnesses. As Winston Churchill once said (he was speaking of Russia), "It is a riddle wrapped in a mystery inside an enigma." Don't leave it to guesswork — find out whether you are having food reactions.

Celiac disease and gluten intolerance are often thought of as rare diagnoses. They tend not to be part of the equation in most medical doctors' considerations, even though they can be the most common denominator. Gluten-related illnesses are very common and very insidious.

Some studies have estimated that close to 40 percent of the population is gluten intolerant (that is almost half the population!) and may develop a myriad of other health conditions if they continue to go undiagnosed.

Autoimmune Disease – The War Within

A healthy immune system functions by releasing white blood cells, which are the troops that defend our body against invading bacteria and potentially harmful infections. In autoimmune diseases, it is a civil war. Acting inappropriately, the immune system begins to attack its own cells. In the case of celiac disease, ingesting gluten triggers the immune system to damage or destroy the villi that line the small intestine. The villi are needed to make enzymes and to absorb nutrients from food. When any amount of gluten is eaten, the result is undigested protein particles. In response to these proteins, the white blood cells, like an army gone awry, attack the villi and microvilli, causing the villi to flatten. Damage to the microvilli leads to nutrition-deficiency syndromes.

> It is well documented that autoimmune diseases tend to travel in tandem. That is, if you develop one, you are likely to develop another.... People with one diagnosed autoimmune disease and unexplained symptoms should explore the link with celiac disease.
> — Peter H. R. Green, M.D.

Are My Symptoms Food Related?

According to *Optimal Wellness* by Ralph Golan, M.D., perhaps 50 percent of symptoms seen in doctors' offices are related to food sensitivities. Allergy reactions to food can show up in nearly any organ or part of the body, and can cause any set of symptoms that come from altered function of these tissues or organs.

Here are some telltale signs and symptoms. You may be gluten intolerant or have celiac disease if you have two or more of the following ongoing complaints.

Common Symptoms of Gluten Intolerance

Skin rashes/eczema	Mental instability
Joint pain	Depression
Low energy, tiredness	Anxiety
Chronic fatigue	Feeling "spaced out"
Chronic back pain	Inability to gain weight
Headaches	Inability to lose weight
Migrating numbness and tingling	Developmental delays in children
Stomach bloating/discomfort	Failure to thrive
	Brain fog
Diarrhea	Menstrual problems
Constipation	Infertility

Conditions Associated with Gluten Intolerance

If you have already been diagnosed with one of the following conditions, you may have an underlying gluten sensitivity that has been overlooked. I strongly recommend getting a stool test.

Irritable bowel syndrome	Psychological stress
Chronic fatigue syndrome	Schizophrenia
Fibromyalgia	Attention deficit disorder
Anemia	Lactose intolerance
Any autoimmune disease	Hypoglycemia
Diabetes	Gastric reflux
Osteoporosis	Thyroid disorders

Sources: *Celiac Disease: A Hidden Epidemic* by Dr. Peter H. Green, Celiac. com, and *Full of It! The Shocking Truth About Gluten* by Dr. Rodney Ford

The following is a brief explanation of some conditions commonly associated with gluten intolerance.

Anemia

When there is damage to the intestinal villi there will be malabsorption of iron, protein, folate, and B12. This leads to anemia.

Irritable Bowel Syndrome

Your intestines aren't in a bad mood. They're most likely irritable because something you're eating is creating inflammation in the gut. Food intolerances are the most likely culprit. If you've been told that you have this condition, get tested for gluten and lactose intolerance. If someone you know is going through this, suggest they get tested, too — you might save a life.

Diabetes

The rate and prevalence of type 2 diabetes, especially in adults, is increasing at an alarming rate. According to the American Diabetes Association, about 41 million Americans are pre-diabetic. Dr. Mercola states that diabetes has increased 700% in the past fifty years. Celiac disease is a hidden epidemic, going silently undiagnosed in millions at the same time that diabetes is increasing at an alarming rate. What is the connection?

According to Dr. Peter H. R. Green, "The association between type 1 or insulin-dependent diabetes mellitus (IDDM) and celiac disease has been recognized for more than forty years." Approximately ten percent of diabetics are also found to have celiac disease. But most diabetics have never been screened for celiac disease or gluten antibodies. Eating excess gluten in people who are genetically sensitive to it may be contributing to the development of diabetes. Everyone has heard of diabetes, or knows someone who has it. Celiac disease is almost as common, but is the most under-diagnosed autoimmune disease of our time. Diabetes is now categorized as an autoimmune disease and the cause of damage to the pancreas is either an autoimmune reaction or sometimes a virus. It is likely that an antibody attack on the pancreas is triggered by both excess sugar and excess gluten, especially since these two sweet poisons are usually eaten together. In cases of diabetes, the blood sugar and insulin regulation are being addressed, but the gluten component is not. According to Dr. Green:

Some physicians have advocated the screening of all diabetics for celiac disease. There is evidence that treating celiac disease will prevent diabetes.

Which came first? Often, celiac disease or gluten intolerance remain the silent causative factors that go undiagnosed until a more serious condition develops. Since there is evidence that treating celiac disease (removing gluten from the diet) can prevent diabetes, all those with risk factors should be screened. Other autoimmune conditions have been associated with gluten intolerance. For example, when gluten targets the joints, it triggers pain and inflammation that lead to rheumatoid arthritis. In autoimmune thyroiditis, the thyroid gland is attacked and there can be a gluten autoimmune association. It is essential to find out before it's too late, because once you have a disease like type 1 diabetes it is irreversible. It is, however, preventable. We need to screen *all* children for gluten intolerance and celiac disease, especially those with a family history of diabetes or autoimmune conditions. Anything less than screening is negligent and a travesty.

Fibromyalgia

By definition this is "pain in the muscle fibers," the diagnosis usually given when no medical reason for muscle pain and fatigue can be found. If you have muscle and joint pain, find out what the underlying cause is. Gluten intolerance and celiac disease cause massive inflammation in the gut that can develop into pain in muscles and joints. Get tested.

Chronic Fatigue

Nothing will make you more tired than a lack of nutrients, unregulated blood sugar, poor absorption, anemia, or chronic immune stress. Wonder why you are always tired? Get tested.

Psychological Conditions

Serotonin is the neurotransmitter your brain needs to feel happy, optimistic, and relaxed. Millions of people experience the many symptoms of low serotonin. According to Dr. John Gray, there is an epidemic of serotonin deficiency, especially in women, resulting in depression and mood disturbances. Serotonin deficiency can cause depression, anxiety, irritability, negativity, dissatisfaction, and feelings of overwhelm.

Countless Americans take medications like Prozac to make up for a lack of serotonin. Low levels of serotonin can come from a lack of proper absorption of nutrients. If you aren't digesting protein or absorbing food properly, you cannot make serotonin. This is often a result of an gluten proteins damaging the gut. When the vital proteins and essential amino acids can't be absorbed, there are no raw materials from which to produce hormones and neurotransmitters. Women have three times the incidence of gluten intolerance and three times the incidence of autoimmune disease. They are also far more likely to become malnourished, get depressed, and seek out psychological help such as therapy. There is a connection. It's not in your head, it's in the bread!

Skin Lesions

Eczema and psoriasis are very common skin ailments, both of which are manifestations of celiac disease and gluten intolerance. The condition of very itchy skin eruptions called dermatitis herpetiformis is often called celiac of the skin. The skin is your body's largest organ. It lives and breathes, and its condition is a reflection of your intestinal health.

Infertility

It can be heartbreaking for couples to be faced with infertility. One of the leading causes of unexplained infertility is undiagnosed celiac disease or gluten intolerance. Pregnancy is a time when a woman's need for calories and nutrients doubles in order to feed a developing baby. If there is undiagnosed celiac disease or gluten intolerance, absorption of food will be hindered. Sometimes ovulation stops when a woman doesn't have adequate nutrient absorption; the body senses that there aren't sufficient nutrients to sustain a pregnancy. This may result in infertility. Even if pregnancy can be achieved, often the fetus may not be adequately nourished. Deficiencies in folic acid and amino acids from malabsorption can lead to miscarriage and birth defects. Removing gluten from your diet may restore fertility.

Our Organs – What They Do and What Goes Wrong– Getting Technical –

The Liver

The liver is the largest internal organ, and it acts as a giant filter to detoxify the blood. If this filter is congested or overworked by inflammation and reactions to gluten toxicity, it can become damaged. If you are intolerant to gluten, eating it can clog up your liver.

In traditional Chinese medicine, every organ has an energy meridian (channel, or pathway) and an emotion associated with it. The liver is the organ of anger, frustration, and resentment. A congested liver can present as a very short-tempered individual who tends toward rage. Such a person can also tend to feel too warm, becoming overheated — literally and figuratively. While drugs and alcohol are more obvious toxins to the liver, gluten is in many cases the hidden source of liver dysfunction.

Consuming gluten when you have an immunologic reaction to that protein can lead to liver damage. Research has found that many cases of serious liver disease and liver failure result from unrecognized celiac disease or gluten intolerance. There are extra-intestinal manifestations of celiac disease as well, meaning that other organs, such as the liver, may be impaired when a gluten-intolerant person eats any gluten at all. Fatty liver or cirrhosis can be a sign of silent celiac disease, even in the absence of digestive symptoms. Studies have shown that liver enzymes can normalize after only six months on a gluten-free diet. Patients on liver-transplant waiting lists have been seen to heal enough on a gluten-free diet that they no longer need a transplant and can be taken off the list.

Pancreas

The pancreas has two main functions: one is to make insulin; the other is to make digestive enzymes. Pancreatic enzymes are secreted into the first part of the small intestines, where all digestion takes place. When there is damage to the villi in the small intestines, the receptor sites for the pancreatic enzymes are affected. The enzymes can't function properly because damage to the villi alters the feedback to the pancreas. This causes an inadequate enzyme supply to be produced, and then digestion halts (and we bloat or get gas). Similarly, insulin production can be too high or too low due to pancreatic problems, which can lead to blood sugar issues such as hyperglycemia or hypoglycemia. Diabetes is the condition in which the pancreatic insulin production is insufficient. This has been shown to be associated with gluten-induced damage to the intestines and pancreas. In Chinese medicine, the emotions associated with the pancreas are worry, nervousness, and hopelessness.

Sugar Stress

When we don't absorb our nutrients properly we crave sugar and sweets to raise our blood glucose. Sugar is an addictive substance. The combination of flour and sugar puts a double load on our system, stressing our pancreas and intestines and putting us in an unstable mental and physical state.

The most harmful sugars are high-fructose corn syrup and processed white sugar. Your best choices for sweeteners are stevia (a naturally sweet herb in the sunflower family), agave nectar, maple syrup, blackstrap molasses, honey, or rapadura (dehydrated cane-sugar juice).

Small Intestine

The small intestine, where our digestion and absorption of nutrients occurs, is approximately twenty-two feet long. It is lined with villi, tiny finger-like projections containing a brushy border called microvilli, which increase the surface area for absorption. In classic celiac disease, the villi are destroyed by an autoimmune reaction to gluten. With destruction of the villi, there is impaired absorption, which leads to vitamin and mineral deficiencies.

Long-term imbalances in the small intestine can cause a person to experience the emotions associated with abandonment, insecurity, and loss.

Adrenal Glands

The adrenal glands are located above each kidney. They are our stress-managing glands, and make hormones such as adrenaline and sex hormones. When we are overloaded with stress — physical, emotional or chemical — the adrenal glands can become overwhelmed. Consumption of coffee, sugar, alcohol and gluten are major stressors to the adrenal glands. Chronic stress from an improper diet or autoimmune disease can cause adrenal fatigue which shows up with a myriad of symptoms, the most common being: exhaustion, dizziness, back pains, anxiety, allergies, insomnia, shakiness, hypoglycemia, moodiness, headaches, and asthma, to name a few.

Most medical doctors are trained to look for disease and not dysfunction. It is fairly rare to find a metabolic disease of the adrenal gland like Addison's disease where there is total failure of the adrenal gland to produce hormones.

However, it is extremely common in today's society to find

adrenal stress and dysfunction. Abnormal adrenal functioning is a major cause of fatigue and weakness and is responsible for many other common symptoms. Removing the chemical stressors like gluten, sugar, alcohol and caffeine can allow the adrenal glands to begin healing.

Thyroid Gland

The thyroid gland is located in the front of the neck. The thyroid is an important endocrine gland that manufactures hormones that control metabolism and growth.

Autoimmune stress to the thyroid gland can cause fatigue, weight loss or weight gain, nervousness, panic attacks, or metabolic disease like thyroiditis, Hashimoto's or Grave's disease. Any autoimmune thyroid issues may have a gluten-intolerance association.

Ileocecal Valve

The ileocecal valve is the doorway that separates the small and large intestine. It is located in the right lower abdomen, two thirds of the way from the belly button toward the top of the right hip bone (right iliac crest). The ileocecal valve is instrumental in dividing the functions of the small and large intestines; the valve acts to keep our kitchen and compost areas separate. Nutrients are fully absorbed in our small intestine before the valve allows them to be released to the large intestine where wastes are eliminated. If the ileocecal valve becomes irritated and swollen by food reactions, it may get stuck open, thus allowing waste products to be reabsorbed and nutrients to be lost. Chronic pain, swelling, or pressure in the right lower belly, in the ileocecal area, is a significant and telling sign of gluten intolerance. Removal of gluten is essential in these cases. An open ileocecal valve requires a bland diet: removal of gluten, caffeine, and spicy and sharp foods like popcorn, nuts, and potato chips.

Allergy vs. Intolerance

Allergies

Allergens are usually proteins, and are substances we come into contact with that create an allergic reaction. Our bodies produce antibodies, which are also proteins, in response to allergens. The specific antibody produced in response to an allergy is immuno-globulin IgE. Histamines are also released when we have allergies, and this is usually a rapid response. For example, with allergies, you may breathe in dust, pollen, or pet dander and have an immediate reaction of sneezing, wheezing, runny nose, or itchy eyes.

Intolerance

When someone has food intolerance, the body also has an immune reaction, but it does not respond with IgE.

Often, it takes longer for the symptoms to appear, which makes it difficult to see the connection between the offensive substance and the complaints. Unlike allergies, which are swift, intolerances often have a delayed reaction; it may take a number of hours or days for the symptom to manifest after the exposure.

Intolerances can also cause an alarming variety of symptoms: stomach problems and GI distress, skin complaints, itching, joint problems, pain and aches, fatigue, asthma, mental stress, depression, headaches, and hypoglycemia, to name a few.

Gluten is a protein allergen. Gluten intolerance often goes undiagnosed because there is a delay in the reaction after eating these flour-based foods, which masks the link between the offending food and the ailment or distress. The immune reactions and nutritional deficiencies that occur over time can become chronic health disturbances.

CHAPTER 5:

This Is Your
Brain on Gluten

Say No to All White Powders

It is interesting that so many comfort foods are carbohydrates. Cookies, pies, muffins, brownies, pasta, breads, and cereals are loaded with gluten flour and sugar. They are both comforting us and killing us. Sugar and flour are as addictive as drugs; in fact, new research has shown that refined sugar is more addictive than cocaine. Most of us know better than to use white-powder drugs such as cocaine and heroine, but we eat flour and sugar regularly. Daily consumption of gluten and sugar becomes very addictive and then takes a huge toll on our health.

You can't go anywhere in this country without being tempted by cake, cookies, brownies, breads, muffins, and such. It's time to just say no to white powders of all kinds. White flour is nothing more than wheat flour that has been bleached. Gluten and sugar are the gateway drugs — insidious, readily available addictive substances that are deadly. If you are "using" regularly, you'll probably end up needing more pharmaceuticals or consuming alcohol to ease the pain and the effects on your nervous system. Eating like this will degenerate your brain.

Addiction and Allergy

We are often drawn to our allergens, which become our addictions. Addiction is closely associated with allergies; the body can become so used to consuming substances like wheat and sugar that withdrawal symptoms may occur when they are removed.

Everybody has a threshold to gluten and sugar. When you exceed this threshold of tolerance, your body becomes more sensitive to these substances and develops allergies, intolerances, or immune reactions to them.

According to Dr. Rodney Ford, in *Full of it! The Shocking Truth About Gluten*, "Gluten has a morphine-like activity. This makes gluten addictive."

> The gluten protein is broken down in your body by gut enzymes into the smaller fragments called peptides. Some of these peptides are known as gluteomorphines: they have a morphine-like activity.

In certain people, these gluteomorphines will target specific receptor sites in the brain, giving you a temporary high that becomes addictive.

Have you ever tried to eat just one cookie?

Psychiatric Disorders, or "Am I Going Crazy?"

Perhaps the most fascinating discovery in current research is the clear association between psychological distress, mental illness, and undiagnosed celiac disease.

Untreated patients with celiac disease or gluten intolerance are often told, "It's all in your head." This is because their symptoms are often chronic, vary greatly, and may present as depression, anxiety, or nervousness. Since wheat is so prevalent in our society, almost all the foods we eat contain some gluten. Our brains are constantly bombarded by these indigestible proteins. Even if you think you're avoiding wheat and gluten, there are many hidden sources like soy sauce and veggie burgers. Celiac and gluten-intolerant sufferers have a significantly higher incidence of behavioral disorders, including depression, bipolar disorder, ADHD, and mental illnesses.

People with celiac disease and other autoimmune disorders are at increased risk of psychiatric problems. In the March 2006 issue of the American Journal of Psychiatry, researchers reported having found that "patients with a history of an autoimmune disorder had a 45% increased risk for schizophrenia." A drastic reduction or total elimination of schizophrenic symptoms has been observed when these patients are put on a gluten-free diet.

I can testify from personal experience, as well as years of seeing patients, that untreated autoimmune disease can manifest itself as mental instability. When your immune system begins to attack your own tissues, you can literally feel like you are turning on yourself. In addition to the physiological effects, a sense of self-loathing and anxiety can accompany an autoimmune reaction. During the two years prior to my diagnosis, I was having daily panic attacks. These became so terrifying that I was prescribed anti-seizure medication. I know now that my physical and emotional imbalances were directly connected. I fed the fire of this autoimmune disease with bread, pasta, pizza, and cookies while my mental state deteriorated and I felt like I was losing control of my mind.

Brain Chemistry Imbalances — Look to the Gut

Whenever a gluten-intolerant person consumes gluten foods, the intestinal lining becomes damaged. Intestinal damage leads to a lack of absorption of essential vitamins, minerals, and amino acids. This will result in deficiencies in the body's ability to produce serotonin and other neurotransmitters needed to keep the brain and the mind balanced.

The brain needs food every minute! The brain makes up 3 percent of the body's weight, but uses 70 percent of the glucose energy. An autoimmune reaction to gluten creates inflammation in the gut that will damage the digestive enzymes, and without these enzymes, normal absorption of nutrients is not possible. Malabsorption leads to malnutrition. The amino acid tryptophan is a precursor to serotonin. When there is deficient absorption of amino acids like tryptophan, there will be inadequate serotonin production. Serotonin is the brain neurotransmitter responsible for feelings of happiness and well-being. When serotonin levels are low, we experience depression, anxiety, and worry, and we may feel overwhelmed. According to Dr. John Gray, author, psychologist, and brain chemistry researcher, there is an epidemic of serotonin deficiency in American women. Millions take psychoactive medications to stimulate serotonin production instead of eating properly and producing it naturally. The pineal gland converts serotonin into melatonin, which is needed for a good night's sleep. Insomnia too can be a nutritional problem.

Whenever there is malabsorption, other neurotransmitters such as dopamine and GABA may become deficient as well, and this can contribute to other psychological problems. Without adequate neurotransmitters, nervousness, anxiety, panic attacks, mental illness, and even seizures may occur.

Dr. John Gray says that talking to a therapist can sometimes be an expensive alternative to eating a healthy breakfast. I would add that a healthy and gluten-free breakfast, lunch, and dinner may save you lots of money in therapy. A diet consisting of whole food — proteins, vegetables, fruit, beans, and rice — will provide you the raw materials to produce serotonin. I spent untold hours talking with therapists and psychologists because I felt emotionally and chemically unstable. It is helpful to talk out your feelings and problems, but it's not the cure if what you're eating is creating the crisis. By getting off gluten, you may discover that your symptoms are not in your head, but in your diet.

Unstable Blood Sugar Leads to Unstable Brain Chemistry

Gluten-intolerant people with unstable blood chemistry will often be drawn to dysfunctional relationships. Among the ways that gluten intolerance affected my brain was my choices in love relationships. At twenty-one I fell in love with and married a man with substance-abuse problems. My marriage was erratic, and my husband was consistently inconsistent, which was right in stride with my fluctuating biochemistry. When it's common to feel chaos in your mind and body, you may be drawn to someone who will recreate that unsettling experience. If you have gluten sensitivities that have led to disturbed biochemistry, the bottom line is that your mind just isn't clear enough to make rational, healthy decisions.

The truth is that eating too much gluten and sugar can make you an emotional mess. If you or someone you know is suffering psychological symptoms or mental instability, I strongly recommend the test for gluten sensitivity (see chapter 6: How To Get Tested). Don't let your mind fall victim to an overlooked and very common dietary imbalance that has a simple, practical solution.

CHAPTER 6:

How To Get Tested

Who Should Be Tested?

I believe that everyone should be tested for gluten intolerance. Certainly anyone with ongoing symptoms or a health condition is urged to get screened for gluten sensitivity. A partial list of people who would benefit from being tested includes those who have joint pain, fatigue, weakness, nerve pain, osteoporosis, infertility, miscarriages, menstrual irregularities, depression, nervousness, panic attacks, any kind of bowel or stomach problems, constipation, diarrhea, bloating in the belly, itchy skin lesions that don't go away, liver disease, diabetes, Crohn's disease, lupus, any other autoimmune diseases, and children with ADD, behavioral, or developmental problems.

Teenagers

I've seen it all too often: the difficult, rebellious teenager is outwardly manifesting an inner gluten intolerance. It's challenging to be in harmony with the world during the hormone-surging years, but even more so for the fourteen-year-old experiencing a daily autoimmune reaction that is literally tearing him or her apart inside with every slice of pizza.

It is important to test the difficult, irritable, fatigued, highly emotional, or reactive kids, and to test the teens who don't exercise or apply themselves. This can be because of pain, weakness, or fatigue. They may be too embarrassed to tell you about their bowel troubles, so they just wear black clothing and listen to weird music.

Getting Tested – It Starts at Home

Enterolab.com

The best lab that I have found for accurately diagnosing both celiac disease and gluten intolerance is called Enterolab, located in Dallas, Texas. Testing is simple: use the Internet to order the stool-sample test kit, which will be sent to your home. You can ship the sample directly from your home back to the lab. The founder of Enterolab, Dr. Kenneth Fine, is a gastroenterologist who has dedicated his entire medical career to researching nutrition, food sensitivities, and inflammatory intestinal disease. Dr. Fine has developed new diagnostic tests for intestinal malabsorption syndromes to identify immune reactions to gluten proteins. Enterolab stool testing is done to measure antibodies and autoimmune reactions to gluten and lactose, as well as providing genetic testing for these conditions.

Stool Tests – Three Simple Steps

No doctor's prescription is necessary to get a stool test. You can order a test kit online; it will be sent to your home, where you can take the test for gluten and lactose sensitivity in the privacy of your own bathroom.

1. Go online to www.enterolab.com, click on ORDER TESTS, follow the prompts for first-time order, and choose GLUTEN SENSITIVITY STOOL AND GENE PANEL COMPLETE. The stool-sample kit will be mailed to you.

2. Following the instructions they provide, take the two samples they need. One sample is taken using the enclosed wooden stick to swab the inside of your cheek. The other is a stool sample. Deposit one bowel specimen in the container provided.

3. Call the 800 number for the lab courier to pick up the samples at your door. It's best to take the sample on a Monday, Tuesday, or Wednesday for ease of shipping.

In two weeks you'll receive an E-mail with results and interpretations of your tests.

The results from Enterolab will tell you if you are gluten sensitive, gluten intolerant, or have celiac disease. They will also show antibody levels against gluten, and whether you possess the genes for either condition, since it is genetic in nature. The test will indicate if you are having an autoimmune reaction to gluten, which means organ damage is occurring. And it tests for lactose intolerance as well. Enterolab provides you a phone number so you can discuss your results with someone at the lab.

How do you know if a child is suffering from gluten intolerance?

▲ *Any child who is always grumpy, has temper tantrums, or is uncomfortable and fussy should be tested.*

▲ *Any child with chronic and reoccurring infections or skin rashes.*

▲ *Any child with stomach aches, a bloated belly or bowel issues (loose stools or difficulty pooping).*

▲ *The child with Attention Deficient Disorder should be tested.*

▲ *Any child with failure to thrive, stunted growth, learning disabilities or brain fog.*

Getting Your Kids Tested

Celiac disease and gluten intolerance are genetic disorders, which means they run in families. The most commonly affected people are of northern European descent. In Italy, where the percentage of celiac disease is high, all children are screened for this disease by the age of five. This is an excellent idea, since the Italians eat a large amount of pasta and bread. In Sweden, an epidemic of celiac disease was observed over ten-year period from the mid-1980s to the mid-'90s. Since then, Sweden has banned gluten from breakfast cereals due to overwhelming research about it, and has seen a radical decline in celiac disease.

Kids in America are being brought up on exactly the foods that are most detrimental to their health. Bagels, cereals, muffins, cookies, sandwiches, pizza, and processed junk foods are contributing to the nation's healthcare crisis. Childhood obesity, juvenile-onset diabetes, ADHD, and learning disabilities are all on the rise. It may be your children's food, not their heads, that creates the imbalance. Should we medicate our children, or should we change their diet?

It makes sense to screen every child for this condition, to provide a dietary guideline for children's nutrition, and hopefully prevent health problems and long-term side effects. Celiac and gluten-intolerant children have been shown to suffer from all sorts of behavioral problems, ADD, failure to thrive, learning problems, irritability, and separation anxiety. Also, children with seizures and autism have shown improvement on a gluten-free diet. If you want your children to grow, learn, remember, and thrive *do not* feed them boxed cereals, breads, bagels, muffins, and pancakes. Cereal grains not only contain toxic gluten, but are also very high in sugar.

Blood Tests

Blood tests are usually the medical doctor's choice for testing for celiac disease. Blood tests can identify celiac disease but are not as accurate for detecting gluten intolerance. Blood tests have a high percentage of false negatives. People with gluten sensitivities and syndromes associated with celiac disease may have a negative blood test but still be intolerant to gluten. This is called gluten intolerant enteropathy, and although it is not textbook celiac disease, the treatment is the same. This requires a strict gluten free diet to improve symptoms and prevent damage to organs. If you have celiac disease, by definition you are gluten intolerant. However, even a greater number of people are gluten intolerant and do not have celiac disease.

Medical Tests for Celiac Disease

Your medical doctor may choose to do blood tests for celiac disease. A celiac blood panel would consist of IgA antibodies, IgA tissue transglutaminase, IgG tissue transglutaminase, and Total IgA antibodies. A positive result indicates celiac disease. A negative result does not rule out celiac disease, however, since there are many false negatives. Blood tests from anti-gliadin antibodies would indicate gluten intolerance, but the stool tests are more comprehensive. The medical gold standard for celiac disease is an intestinal biopsy demonstrating flattened or damaged villi in the small intestine. A positive biopsy result gives the diagnosis of celiac disease. A negative result does not rule out celiac, however, since there can be false negatives with biopsies. A biopsy takes tiny pieces of the small intestine to examine. Since the intestines are many feet long, the section biopsied can miss the portion of the intestine that is being affected. Also, a biopsy looks only for intestinal damage, when it may be other organs that are being damaged by gluten reactions.

Celiac Disease or Gluten Intolerance – Genetic Markers

There are specific tests to see if you have the genes for celiac disease. The genetic markers are (HLA DQ 2,8). There is also a specific genetic test for gluten sensitivity (HLA DQ 1,3). If you possess one or two copies of the gluten-sensitive gene, your symptoms will be similar to celiac disease. Until very recently there was no way to get a diagnosis of gluten sensitivity. The stool test has made it possible to identify autoimmune gluten intolerance. Remember: if left untreated, gluten sensitivity/intolerance can progress to intestinal damage and a wide array of absorption and other problems similar to celiac disease.

Celiac disease and diabetes are both associated with the same genetic markers (HLA DQ 2,8).

Why Test Stool?

The stool will contain all the inflammatory markers and antibodies, if any are present. About 90 percent of our immune system is located in our intestines. When testing for food sensitivities, these reactions occur in the intestines, not in the blood. The end waste product of the war within the gut is our feces. If your doctor runs a celiac blood panel and it is negative, consider a stool test before you give up. Stool tests are better at revealing gluten sensitivities than blood tests are.

Do I have to eat gluten before my stool test?

No. Another reason the stool test is preferable is that there's no need to reintroduce gluten into your diet, even if you've been off it for a few months. (If you've been off gluten for six months or longer you may have a negative stool test result. If there is no exposure, there will be no more antibody reaction). With blood tests, you need to be currently eating gluten. For those who've been off of gluten for a little while and know the consequences eating it again, this can be unbearable.

Additionally, stool tests are non-invasive and can be done in the privacy of your home. Also, there are a large percentage of false negatives from the blood tests (more than 30 percent of people with confirmed celiac disease have negative blood tests). **It's very important to remember that stool tests can identify gluten intolerance or celiac disease, while blood tests only test for celiac disease.**

Although I highly recommend the stool test, so you know just how seriously to take this diet, I realize that many people simply can't afford the cost.* You can begin the elimination diet and use your symptoms as your guidelines.

Elimination Diet

Before you accept any diagnosis, decide to resign yourself to feeling sick, think that you've gone crazy, or live on an abundance of medications, try an elimination diet. Take gluten completely out of your diet for thirty days. Totally avoid bread, pizza, pasta, and baked goods. **Do not cheat** — don't eat one cookie or cracker unless it's a gluten-free brand. Follow this diet carefully for one month and watch how your body responds. You might be amazed at how much lighter you feel, how pain melts away, and how your energy increases.

This is your own personal study. It consists of one subject — you. You don't have to wait for further research or lab-test results (though I highly recommend the stool analysis first). To truly experience your body gluten free and see whether you're one of the millions who are wheat/gluten intolerant, try the elimination diet. When you go off gluten for thirty days, be very strict; follow the guidelines in "What Can I Eat?" (see chapter 7). To be safe during the first month, try to cook most meals at home. Write down all your symptoms before you start. Then remove the gluten from your diet and observe your body. After a few weeks it may feel like you have new lease on life. After thirty gluten-free days you may be convinced and feel inspired to go off gluten forever. If you have children, provide them a gluten-free diet simultaneously.

---

* Stool tests cost approximately $350.

The Good News

The intestinal microvilli that are damaged by gluten reactions can regenerate. If you maintain a gluten-free diet, most of the damaged villi will renew rapidly, will actively absorb nutrients again, and you will feel better! Depending on how long your gluten intolerance has gone untreated, and the extent of the damage, it may take six months to a year to reverse the damage in your intestines.

If you have been recently diagnosed, I suggest that you let yourself grieve. There may be denial and resistance in the beginning. You may be angry or feel deprived. Your liver may be mad as well, agitated by inflammation from all of those poisons. Our bodies' dis-ease can manifest as emotional symptoms. Feel it all. Do your grieving. Then get over it. You'll get your health back and life after bread will be better. If you're a carbohydrate addict, no doctor can fix you. Recovery is ultimately up to you, not your physician.

CHAPTER 7

The Gluten-free Diet

To Eat or Not to Eat:
Changing Your Diet
and Saving Your Life

Read all food labels. Just because food appears on the shelf doesn't mean it's safe and we should buy it. Look for GLUTEN-FREE on the label, or buy whole foods — meats, fish, eggs, fruits, and vegetables — instead of processed foods that come in boxes. Treat going to the grocery store as you would a trip to the library for research.

What Contains Gluten and What Not to Eat

Avoid wheat, rye, barley, and all foods containing these ingredients — they all contain gluten:

Barley malt, wheat starch, semolina, bulgur, couscous, farina, durum, flour, matzoh, spelt, kamut, triticale, and beer. Most all baked goods — breads, pasta, pizza, muffins, cookies, rolls, croissants, cakes, and waffles. White flour (bleached wheat flour). Most boxed cereals and granola. Bagels are the most glutenous thing on earth — avoid them like the plague.

Foods that are breaded, floured, or served in a sauce prepared with wheat.

Flour tortillas, phyllo dough, things with crusts.

Most soy sauces and oyster sauces contain wheat.

Many marinades contain wheat (read the labels!).

Avoid licorice, jellybeans, and jelly candies — they all contain wheat. Gummy bears are gluten bears!

Seitan is wheat meat — stay away!

Read salad-dressing labels: beware of soy sauce — it contains wheat.

In the beginning it might feel like you're tiptoeing around land mines. Gluten is all around you, and you don't know where it's safe to turn. There are some risky foods. Meats and vegetables prepared at restaurants may be marinated in soy sauce (a fermented wheat and soy mixture) or oyster sauce (very common in Asian cuisine), and are unsafe. Ask restaurants about their sauces and marinades. Oats are controversial. Oats and oatmeal are often contaminated with wheat since they're processed in the same bins in factories. Oats produced in a gluten-free environment are safe. Read the product label or call the company. There are now suppliers of gluten-free oats. Steel-cut oats are the safest, but avoid quick oats. Imitation crabmeat, seasoning packets, some pharmaceuticals, and processed yogurt that contains granola also may contain gluten. Some herbal tea blends are sweetened with barley malt, so read those labels. Soy or veggie burgers are often wheat meat, so say no!

What Can I Eat? Safe Foods

Here are just some of the great foods you can eat:

- *All plain protein: Beef, chicken, fish, eggs, turkey, buffalo, pork*
- *Dairy: Cheese (plain and unseasoned are gluten free and safe)*
- *Vegetables — all are gluten free!*
- *Fruits are gluten free*
- *Beans*
- *Nuts*

The safe grains are rice, corn, amaranth, quinoa, millet, sorghum, and buckwheat (although the name sounds glutenous, buckwheat is gluten free if no wheat has been mixed into it.) You can use butter, milk, olive oil, and most vinegars. Tamari is soy sauce made without wheat. Soybeans and plain tofu are also gluten free. Quinoa flakes make a great high-protein, gluten-free oatmeal. Corn flakes are usually a safe cereal if no wheat or barley malt has been added.

Additives – Are They Safe?

All of the following ingredients are gluten free and safe: glucose syrup, lecithin, oat gum, food starch, plain spices, cornstarch, arrowroot, xanthan gum, tapioca flour, rice flour, almond flour, potato flour, and potato starch.

Whole Foods Market has a great gluten-free bakery, delicious breads, pizza crusts, and muffins made with rice and almond flours. Pamela's Products makes an awesome gluten-free pancake and baking mix. Find a health-food store and imagine you're on a treasure hunt to find the best gluten-free products available. Glutino makes a variety of great breads, cookies, and pizza crusts.

Questionable Additives

Dextrin – *an incompletely hydrolyzed starch derived from corn, potato, rice, or wheat. This requires investigation; call the manufacturer if the label doesn't provide the source.*

Malt or malt flavoring – *unsafe because it's from barley malt or syrup, which contain gluten.*

Maltodextrin – *these two words together are safe in the US because the word requires that the product be made from corn.*

Hydrolyzed vegetable protein (HVP) or textured vegetable protein – *this can be made form soy, corn, rice, or wheat, and is commonly found in canned soups, sausages, hot dogs, and vegetarian meats. Check with the manufacturer to learn the source.*

Glutinous rice – *sounds bad, but it's safe. Glutinous means sticky (containing gluten would be glutenous).*

Multiple Food Reactions

Many celiacs and individuals with gluten intolerance have other food sensitivities as well. Dairy, soy, and nuts can be difficult to digest for those whose intestines have been impaired. Members of the nightshade family, such as tomatoes, peppers, potatoes, and eggplant may also cause symptoms. This may be only temporary, until the intestines heal.

Lactose Intolerance – the Cheese that Binds

All dairy products such as cheese are gluten free, but people with gluten intolerance commonly have lactose intolerance as well. This is because the enzyme lactase, which is needed to digest milk and other dairy products, is produced in the microvilli of the small intestine. When there is damage to the intestinal lining, there is loss of digestive enzymes.

If you have primary lactose intolerance, it means you genetically lack the enzyme lactase to digest milk, cheese, butter, and other dairy products. This affects about 25 percent of the US population. Often, people with gluten intolerance develop a secondary lactose intolerance.

Secondary lactose intolerance can occur whenever there is damage to the microvilli leading to a loss of the enzyme lactase. This is commonly seen in celiac disease, but it can also be caused by parasites or infections in the intestines. As the small intestine heals on a gluten-free diet, enzyme production will return and you may be able to eat dairy products again.

If you have recently been found to be gluten intolerant or celiac, you may need to avoid dairy foods for a while. Some people who've developed secondary lactose intolerance find that is reversible. Throughout my life, eating dairy made me bloat or have discomfort, so I assumed that I was lactose intolerant — a very common belief in undiagnosed celiacs. About six months after getting off of gluten I was pleasantly surprised to find that I was able to digest dairy foods well for the first time in my life. After a few months of not eating gluten, your lactase production may resume, so try slowly reintroducing dairy into you diet and see how your body responds.

Remember that eggs are not a dairy food, even though they're found in the dairy section of the market. They don't come from milk and do not require lactase to digest them. If you're not eating dairy due to lactose intolerance, you can still eat eggs.

Alcohol – Can I Drink to That?

Beer is absolutely unsafe. It is liquefied wheat and barley malt. I now understand why in college I would get horribly sick when I drank even one beer. I couldn't drink beer at parties, the way most students were doing. I quit drinking beer long before I knew about gluten. If drinking beer (even one or two) makes you really sick or gives you instant stomach distress, you are probably gluten intolerant. This liquid gluten will affect your intestines very rapidly.

Gluten-free alcohol: Wine, (the healthiest choice), sake (rice wine), tequila (made from cactus), brandy, rum, and cognac.

Questionable: Alcoholic beverages distilled from grain – there is controversy regarding whether the distillation process yields gluten in the end product. The original mash (from wheat, rye, barley, or other grains) may be added back at the end of the process. To be safe, stick with wine, sake, rum, and tequila (and have a designated driver!).

Healing Starts in the Kitchen

Cooking for yourself at home is the safest way to control the food you eat and thus support your healing process. After my diagnosis, I emptied kitchen cabinets of anything that contained gluten — which turned out to be practically everything. (There was barley-malt sweetener in my herbal tea!) Then I started over. I bought a gluten-free recipe book. I got online and ordered one month's worth of gluten-free foods to sustain me until I could research and shop for the right fresh foods and restock the kitchen. Some of the wheat-containing foods I had to replace were: salad dressings, soy sauce, barbecue sauce/marinades, pasta, waffle mix, and energy bars. I'd been eating "The Zone" nutrition bars, which are wheat free, but they contain barley malt and oats, so they were out.

It's best to start with simple, whole foods: meats, fish, vegetables, fruits, rice, and beans. Eat dairy only if you can tolerate it. Gluten-free flours are available for pancakes, bread, and cookies, and there are pastas made from brown rice. These are all delicious. I remember when the Whole Foods Grocery opened a gluten-free bakery with gluten-free prairie bread and sandwich bread, brownies, pies, and cookies. I thought I had died and gone to gluten-free heaven. Inevitably, I gorged on these for a little while and overdid it. It's best to use these gluten-free flours in moderation while your body is healing. They are often made from nuts, which are nutritious but high in fat, so go slow. Gluten-free cookies still contain sugar, so exercise restraint in enjoying treats. To start with, eat more fresh foods, meats, and vegetables, and less flour.

4 Easy Sample Breakfasts

Fried egg with butter and a side of gluten-free oatmeal
Smoked salmon on gluten-free toast with avocado and tomato
Pamela's gluten-free pancakes with plain yogurt, maple syrup, and fruit
Egg omelet with veggies (onions, tomato, spinach, and squash); add cheese if you can tolerate diary

4 Sample Lunches

Turkey burger patty, no bun, with sliced avocado and a side salad
Grilled chicken on salad with a gluten-free dressing
Brown rice, black beans, and green vegetables
Stir-fried sliced steak, quinoa, and vegetables

4 Dinners

Chicken tacos on corn tortillas with cilantro, lettuce, and salsa
Steak, sautéed kale, and baked potato
Salmon with lemon and butter, polenta, and vegetable
Meat of your choice, vegetables, and sweet potato

Eating Out –
Be a Card-carrying Member

I carry small cards that explain that I have gluten intolerance/celiac disease and will get sick if I ingest gluten. When I eat out, before ordering anything, I give this card to a server or directly to the kitchen staff. Then I ask them what would be safe for me to eat. It is crucial to explain to the hostess, server, or kitchen staff that your food must be gluten free. The card helps relay the message to the food preparers without relying on anyone to have memorized a list of ingredients. I call this my Medical Allergy Card. It looks very official, and most places take it seriously. Such a card can help you take control of your fate when meal preparation is in someone else's hands. You can have your own personalized card made up at any place that prints business cards, or order them online.

Questions to Ask at Restaurants

Staying away from breads, rolls, pasta, pizza, and cookie and cake desserts is the right start. To avoid getting dosed with hidden gluten when you eat out, ask these questions before you order:

+ Do you marinate your meat, chicken, fish, or tofu in soy sauce or oyster sauce? If yes, can you use Tamari or fish sauce instead (both are gluten free), or perhaps no marinade?

+ Do you use flour to thicken your soups or sauces?

+ Do you fry your French fries in the same deep fryer as breaded foods like onion rings or chicken strips?

+ Are there croutons or bread in your salads?

+ Can you use a corn tortilla instead of a flour tortilla?

Sample Card

> ### I HAVE CELIAC DISEASE (Gluten Intolerance)
>
> *I cannot eat wheat, rye, barley, malt, soy sauce,*
> *or breadcrumbs, all of which contain gluten,*
> *and will make me very ill.*
>
> *I am able to eat corn and rice.*
>
> *Please check with the kitchen about these*
> *ingredients so I may eat safely.*
>
> *Thank you.*

Single and Celiac

Newly diagnosed and recently divorced, I found myself single and celiac. Eating was challenging. Eating out while on a date felt like trying to walk a tightrope wearing heels, with my stomach growling.

To weed out anyone who was not "strong enough to be my man" on a first date, which usually involved a meal, I felt the need to tell my story. Prior to ordering, I would tell my date all the details of my illness, the misdiagnoses, and the medications needlessly prescribed. Then, I would repeat a condensed version for the server. If that wasn't enough, I would then tell my date that if he wanted to eat pizza, drink beer, or have children, I was not the woman for him.

I was a doctor recovering from celiac disease and writing a book about the issue. I had a lot to say about it. The mother of one of my dates was pre-diabetic, and another date had a young son with ADD. I felt it was my duty to try to help their relatives with information about gluten stool testing. I became a great resource while dating, but stayed single.

This was my catharsis. I pushed men away before they could reject me as a celiac. After telling my story enough times, I had the "gluten-free dining card" made, and would hand one to the waitperson, saying, "This is a food-allergy card." Some explaining and checking of ingredients would follow. My dinner companion didn't need to know about my CAT scan or MRI. My long battle with depression and intestinal distress didn't need to be discussed on the first date.

I was deeply touched by meeting someone who really got it and embraced me as a gluten-free person. There was an exhilarating sweetness to getting a gift of gluten-free chocolates or rice crackers. My favorite became a home-cooked meal consciously prepared without any offending grains so as to allow me a worry-free evening. My diet is now healthy and balanced despite being restricted, and I enjoy being with people who understand and support me in this area.

Nutritional Supplement Recommendations

Supplements should be tailored to your individual needs. It's helpful to consult an applied kinesiologist, naturopath, holistic doctor, or nutritionist.

One of the easiest ways to improve the quality of your life is by taking a good omega 3 fish oil. Cod liver oil/omega 3 fatty acids are important for the health of brain, nerves, joints, and intestinal lining. I recommend Arctic krill oil, which you can order at www.mercola.com, or Nordic Naturals Arctic cod liver oil.

As you begin your gluten-free diet, here are some recommendations for supplements that are available at most health-food stores:

- *Omega 3 fish oil*
- *L-Glutamine powder – an amino acid that helps heal the intestines; take on an empty stomach*
- *Multivitamin with iron*
- *Calcium and magnesium – malabsorption of calcium can lead to osteoporosis*
- *Licorice tea – helps with hypoglycemia*
- *Wobenzyme – an oral enzyme that has anti-inflammatory properties; it helps reduce pain and inflammation in joints, and aids in digestion.*
- *Milk thistle/dandelion root – cleanses the liver*
- *Digestive enzymes*

Supplements available from Vitamin Research Products
800-877-2447

- **Lithium orotate:** *helps with depression. This is a trace mineral (it's not the pharmaceutical drug prescribed for bipolar disorder). Take one in the morning to boost your mood.*
- **Oregano oil:** *helps eliminate bacteria and fungi from the gut and boosts immunity*
- **Forskolin:** *an Ayurvedic herb that resensitizes cell receptors. This helps communication between cells and is great for hypoglycemia and insulin resistance.*
- **Extend One:** *a great multivitamin*

> ## What to Avoid and Not Eat
>
> - *All gluten grains*
> - *Sodas (including diet)*
> - *Partially hydrogenated oils (cottonseed, soy bean, and safflower)*
> - *High-fructose corn syrup*
> - *MSG, nitrates*
> - *Chlorinated water – don't drink it or swim in it*
> - *Aspartame and other artificial sweeteners*

Accidental Exposure to Gluten

It can be risky to eat in restaurants or go to parties or to potlucks where you have no control over the food preparation. During my first year of being off gluten I was afraid to eat out, worried that I would be accidentally dosed with gluten and feel awful for the next twenty-four hours.

If you have an accidental exposure and begin to feel that familiar distress, there's one remedy that might help. Taking activated charcoal directly after the exposure to gluten can soak up the gluten in your intestines. Activated charcoal blocks the absorption of everything in the gut, including gluten and all other nutrients. Only use this infrequently for accidental exposures, not as an excuse to cheat on the diet. Activated charcoal can be bought at most health-food stores and is good to have on hand. Be aware that it may give you a large, dark bowel movement as the charcoal and everything it has absorbed is eliminated.

Once, I had a first date with someone who knew my condition. We went to a restaurant where they knew me. The waitress brought me the wrong dish, however, and while I was eating I began to feel that old familiar bloating. I asked the manager if she was sure that I'd been given the food with the wheat-free soy sauce. Investigation revealed that "my" dinner was still in the kitchen. Luckily, my date understood the situation; we immediately left the restaurant to find activated charcoal. It became an adventure that made us laugh as we went from the supermarket to the health-food store in search of the remedy before the serious malaise set in. It was quite an unusual first date.

Labeling Laws as of January 2006

The labeling laws now require all packaged food to list the most common allergens. They must say if the food contains: wheat, milk, soy, eggs, peanuts, tree nuts, or shellfish, even in trace amounts. Unfortunately "Gluten" was left off this list of required allergens. (This is a travesty for millions of Americans.) Read all labels and ingredients. Remember that "wheat free" does not always mean "gluten free". Vitamin companies are also required to list these allergens on their bottles. Most good brand supplement companies from the health food store will say they are free of wheat, gluten and soy. Pharmaceutical companies are not required to disclose their binding agents and are not under the labeling laws. (Above the law?) Sometimes wheat based starch is used to hold a pill together (remember that gluten is sticky). If you are taking prescription medication call your pharmacy or the company directly to see if wheat or gluten is used as an inactive ingredient.

Gluten-free Shopping List

This is a good guideline to follow when you go to the grocery store. You will primarily be going down the meat, vegetable, and fruit aisles. Foods to buy:

- **All Protein:** Chicken, fish (salmon, cod, shrimp tuna, halibut), turkey, beef, pork, eggs, soy, tofu, sunshine burgers (made from rice)

- **All beans and legumes:** Black beans, pinto beans, lentils, garbanzo beans, kidney beans, lima beans

- **All vegetables:** Squash, green beans, potatoes, broccoli, carrots, salad mix, artichokes, cucumbers, peppers, onions, garlic, tomatoes, kale, chard, spinach, mushrooms, bok choy

- **All fruit:** Melons, apples, pears, bananas, peaches, nectarines, berries, kiwi, oranges

- **Only these grains:** Rice, corn, quinoa, millet, polenta, and these same grains in the form of rice cakes, rice crackers, rice pasta, rice bread, corn tortillas, brown rice tortillas, quinoa flakes

- **Sauces:** Olive oil, wheat-free tamari, butter, yogurt, cheeses

- **Sweets:** Gluten-free cookies, baking mixes (Pamela's are the best!)

CHAPTER 8

Uncovering the Hidden Epidemic

I want to pay tribute to Dr. Peter H. R. Green, of Columbia University, who in 2006 published *Celiac Disease: A Hidden Epidemic*. In this breakthrough book, Dr. Green states that millions of Americans can end their medical odyssey and get the right diagnosis. According to Dr. Green, "The true medical impact of celiac disease is just starting to emerge." His research shows that celiac disease affects one in every hundred people, making it not only the most common autoimmune condition that exists but also the most under-diagnosed. He also explains that celiac disease can affect any organ—the heart, the ovaries, the pancreas, the skin, and so on. This is clearly not just an intestinal disease, but a multi-system disorder.

Dr. Green estimates that over 3 million Americans have celiac disease but haven't been diagnosed due to poor awareness. (New research now shows that figure to be much higher.) This means that 97 percent of people with the disorder still don't know they have it. Celiac disease is as common as high cholesterol. Gluten-intolerant illnesses affect even more—some estimates say that 10 million Americans have undiagnosed gluten intolerance. It truly is a hidden epidemic.

Recent data shows that 1 in 10 people in the general public have reactions to gluten, and some research estimates are even higher. According to Dr. Rodney Ford:

> I calculate that about 1 in 3 who are chronically unwell might be gluten-sensitive. In other words, I suspect that up to a third of all chronic ailments can be attributed to their adverse reactions to gluten.

Celiac is as common as high cholesterol. You can't throw a bagel in New York without hitting a celiac.

Hide and Go Seek a Celiac

In my work as a holistic doctor, chiropractor, and applied kinesiologist, I've treated thousands of patients with musculoskeletal complaints—muscle and joint pain, headache, back and neck pain, carpal tunnel syndrome, sciatica, and the like. I see two kinds of patients. The first are the people who have pain in one or two areas, especially after repetitive work or an injury. They come to my office with a sore lower back, a stiff neck, or a persistent headache. These patients respond well to adjustments, massage, and acupressure, and they get better quickly. The second kind of patient I see has multiple complaints, often systemic—meaning that the entire system is affected. This is the individual who says, "I hurt all over," "I'm always tired and achy," "I can't exercise because of the pain," "I feel run-down," "I live on ibuprofen," "I have no energy." Bingo! This is the patient I test for gluten-intolerance or celiac disease. In one year I found 107 gluten-intolerant and celiac patients (confirmed by stool tests) in my office complaining of exactly these ailments. It may take one to know one, but this pattern of multi-system problems can be a sign of an autoimmune reaction and/or food sensitivity. Gluten intolerance is a common explanation for many of these people's problems.

The most interesting common finding when a patient gives his or her history is the complaint of pain or injury from exercise. Almost every patient who complained of inability to exercise without straining something or feeling immediate pain and fatigue has tested positive for gluten intolerance or celiac disease. This was my experience as well: I would push myself to work out because of phrases like "no pain, no gain." Well, without eating gluten, I can exercise moderately and feel a healthy amount of soreness. Now, it's more like "No pain—hey, no pain!"

In my practice in Mendocino, California, my focus has shifted from chiropractic treatment of common joint and muscle pain, to food allergies and sensitivities, nutritional testing, and gluten intolerance. I see a great many of these patients now, and this path has provided the missing piece for many who had puzzling unresolved symptoms.

Case Studies

Lacey

A mother brought her sixteen-year-old daughter for a nutritional consultation. Lacey had been adopted as a baby, and her mother stated that Lacey had always been depressed and fatigued. She was lethargic, wore all black, and was despondent. Since the age of three she had seen multiple medical specialists and had been tested for everything under the sun, but no helpful diagnosis had been made. Having concluded that Lacey was clinically depressed, a medical doctor prescribed two antidepressant medications. When Lacey came to my office she had three chief complaints: 1) she was depressed; 2) she couldn't exercise without pain or fatigue; and 3) her back hurt all over.

Using applied kinesiology, I muscle tested Lacey and found that all of her organ points were weak—liver, kidney, pancreas, adrenal, and intestines. She had painful abdominal bloating, especially in the ileocecal valve area, the right lower belly. She also had severe tenderness with just light touch to her spine. I immediately sent her for a gene panel and an Enterolab stool analysis for gluten sensitivity. Her test came back positive—she was severely gluten and lactose intolerant. It made sense that she had been depressed; she had an autoimmune gluten intolerance that was unrecognized by doctors, who told her, essentially, that it was all in her head. She was reluctant at first to try the strict diet, but her mother was determined to help her. Within weeks of going off gluten, Lacey, wearing bright colors, bounced into my office with a new sparkle in her eyes. All of her pain was gone, she was no longer depressed, she had energy to exercise, and she felt relief for the first time. On a gluten-free diet all of her previously weak organ points now tested strong. Her mother said, "My daughter is a new person without gluten."

Sarah

Sarah is a twenty-eight-year-old who came to the office crying. She was nervous, anxious, and distraught. She had recently broken up with her boyfriend. She was thin, weak, depressed, and needy. Her hips and shoulders ached and her stomach was continually upset.

Treated with adjustments and hands-on therapy, Sarah improved a little but not much. She was really suffering. After three months of treatment, Sarah finally agreed to get gluten-sensitivity stool tests, which came back indicating an autoimmune intolerance to gluten that was off the charts. Sarah also had other food sensitivities. She had to go off gluten, dairy, and soy. She's improving both physically and emotionally and is more stable than ever. She says she feels stronger, more balanced, and happier now that she has changed her diet.

Julie

Several years ago I was treating Julie, who came to see me for chiropractic care when she was seventeen. Back then she was chronically spraining her ankles and injuring herself with exercise. Julie really wanted to be an aerobics instructor, but most times when she worked out, she hurt herself. I would adjust her knees and ankles and she would improve, but would soon re-injure herself. A few years passed, Julie went off to college, and I stopped practicing for some months because of ill health. When I was better, Julie returned. She was now twenty, and had recently had to drop out of college because of severe back pain. She was receiving physical therapy but her condition was not improving, and she could no longer exercise. Julie had seen an orthopedist who scheduled her to have back surgery—a laminectomy at L5—in which a piece of the vertebra is removed.

With a good understanding of my own diagnosis by this time, I suspected that Julie had a similar gluten intolerance. She had no digestive symptoms, just severe back pain and inflammation, with a history of weakness and joint sprains on exercise. Julie's stool tests for gluten intolerance were positive and she willingly quit gluten. Within a week's time her back pain was gone and she canceled her surgery. Her father was skeptical; he wanted a medical doctor's opinion and took her to a GI specialist. Julie had no GI symptoms, and her stool-test gene panel was positive for gluten intolerance, not celiac disease. There is no blood test for gluten intolerance. The gastroenterologist did the standard blood tests for celiac disease, which came back negative. By that time Julie had been off gluten for two months, so her doctor recommended that, for the blood test to be accurate, she begin to eat gluten grains again for four to six weeks. Two days after reintroducing gluten into her diet, Julie's back pain returned. She refused to eat any more gluten. Julie is gluten free, back in college, and feeling well—no surgery needed!

Kelley

Kelley is a forty-three-year-old schoolteacher who came to my office complaining of hip and joint pain and of continual tiredness. I adjusted her for a few months, and she would get relief initially, but the pain always returned. Then Kelley mentioned that she had lived in Japan for a year and had had no hip or joint pain during that time. The Japanese diet is mainly fish and rice; Japan is certainly not a gluten-eating country. Kelley and I discussed it, and agreed that gluten sensitivity might be causing her joint pain and fatigue. She had no stomach distress, but we decided to explore it. I muscle tested her for gluten, and she showed a weakness to it. She didn't want to take any lab or stool test right away, so we put her on an exclusion diet—no gluten for two months. Kelley did well. Her hip and joint pain resolved and she had more energy. The most telling experience was when, a couple of months into the diet, she cheated and ate a brownie on her daughter's birthday. The next day she felt like she'd been "hit by a truck." She was in a lot of pain and was exhausted. She noticed that her fatigue and pain were directly related to eating wheat or gluten products. She decided to take the stool tests, which confirmed the diagnosis of gluten intolerance.

Karen

Karen came to my office for a consult; at the age of fifty-five she appeared healthy and physically fit. Her history, however, was she had been diagnosed with adult onset diabetes at age forty-eight.

For the past seven years Karen had been on oral diabetic medication. Her fasting blood sugar was 200 at the time of her diagnosis. Normal fasting blood sugar is 70–100. The oral diabetic medication she had been prescribed brought her fasting blood sugar to 130–140, which is still elevated. No matter what she did, how many endocrinologists she saw, or what drugs they gave her, her fasting blood sugar remained elevated at 130–140. Her endocrinologist told her that she was "on a slippery slope to needing insulin injections," and that in another year or two it would probably come to this.

Karen had heard of my work with food intolerances, and I had recently helped solve a gluten-related problem in her twenty-five-year-old son. Karen came in as a new patient wondering if I could help her with her diet and test her for foods. While I do not treat diabetes, I do treat patients with food intolerances that would lead to these conditions. Upon testing, Karen showed a wheat and gluten sensitivity. She told me that none of her other doctors had ever even mentioned the connection between celiac disease, gluten intolerance, and diabetes. Karen felt she ate a healthy, balanced diet, but it did include gluten every day. She wanted to try the gluten elimination diet right away. Within FOUR DAYS of not eating gluten, Karen's fasting blood sugar was 98. This is lower than it had been in over seven years, even on medications. Within a month of being gluten-free, Karen's energy level came up and her blood sugar stabilized around 90. She told me, "This is a total no-brainer. I feel a thousand percent better. I can't believe no doctor ever told me I could make this diet change to correct my diabetes!"

Carle

A mother brought in her three-year-old girl with chronic skin rashes, ear infections, and bellyaches. The child had already taken four rounds of antibiotics and was still having problems. We determined that Carle had both gluten and lactose intolerance. Her mom diligently removed these foods from her daughter's diet, and within one week Carle's rashes cleared up, her belly stopped hurting, and she became a healthy, happy child.

Mary

Mary came to my office wearing wrist braces on both wrists, and complaining of pain and numbness in both hands. She could barely use a pen or grip a cup. She had been diagnosed with bilateral carpal tunnel syndrome, which she was told would require surgery. Her recent history revealed that within the last year she had had surgery on both knees for ligament sprains and tears. She hadn't experienced any significant traumas. Her knees were not improving, even after surgery and six months of physical therapy. Mary was still experiencing knee pain, lack of motion, weakness, and swelling in the joints.

Anytime someone has bilateral symptoms of pain and inflammation that are non-traumatic (meaning both sides of the body are affected and there has been no direct injury), a red flag goes up in my head. This is systemic inflammation.

I tested Mary in my office, using applied kinesiology. She muscle tested weak for wheat and gluten. I adjusted her wrists and knees and put her on a gluten-free diet. One month following her gluten-free diet she returned to the office and shook my hand firmly. She no longer had pain or numbness in her wrists or hands, and her strength had returned. She also noted that her knees were stronger for the first time since her surgery, with no more pain and swelling.

The Dilemma of the Medical Paradigm

In many visits to medical doctors during my years of suffering, no one ever suggested that poor diet might be upsetting my body chemistry and causing my declining health.

Our medical care system in the US is based on drugs and surgery. Diet and nutrition have little part in the picture, when precisely the opposite focus is needed. Sadly, when patients with food sensitivities seek out medical care, traditional doctors medicate these people rather than educating them about their diet. Food *is* our medicine. Drugs and surgery are disease care, not sustainable healthcare. Traditional medical care looks for diseases, and if no disease has manifested yet, then it's assumed that the patient is healthy. This is preposterous!

True health is not merely the absence of an identifiable disease. Drugs are often given to mask symptoms, which are the signs that something is wrong. We need a more proactive approach. Alternative healthcare is about paying attention to symptoms and using preventative therapies. Many steps occur between healthy, normal body functioning and the development of disease. We all have our particular genetic predispositions, and environmental factors are also at work; however, one thing that we have full control over is our choices regarding nutrition. Food is the fuel we run our bodies on, and what we choose to eat ultimately determines our well-being.

If you don't know that you're gluten intolerant and you eat a bowl of cereal, some toast, or a bagel for breakfast, you will soon feel tired and sluggish as the day progresses. Your stomach may bloat, or you might have pain and bowel problems ranging from constipation to loose, runny stools. Your joints may ache or you might get a headache. Little things may make you feel upset and

irritable or even depressed. By the end of the day you're too tired
to cook dinner, so you do something simple, like order a pizza.
Your condition persists.

Or perhaps your kids start the day with Cocoa Puffs and eat
sandwiches for lunch. By 6 p.m., it appears that your son has ADD
and your daughter can't stop crying. It's a vicious cycle, and only
getting off gluten can stop it.

My Disease Became My Teacher

From a young age I felt that I was different; I could tell that my
body didn't work right. My moods were unpredictable at best. I
experienced my organs malfunctioning. I saw the dysfunction in
the medical doctors and in the healthcare system as a whole. I lived
through the terrible ordeal of nearly starving to death from nutrition deficiencies while being told it was all in my head.

I grew up eating Oreo cookies and Ritz crackers in front of the
T.V. I watched streams of commercials for these types of "foods,"
and figured that if the makers were allowed to advertise these products on television then they must be safe to eat.

Millions of Americans are going through this, ineffectually gorg-
ing themselves on gluten-filled carbohydrates in a futile attempt
to satiate their constant hunger. Then they become sick, fatigued,
overweight, depressed, or mentally unstable.

I believe that this autoimmune condition gave me insight and
increased intuition. My sensitivities were so strong that I now have
an understanding and ability to see what's wrong with people and
how to help heal them. I can put my hands on a patient and intui-
tively get information about their problem. Using muscle testing, I
can identify food intolerance in a patient. Sometimes just hearing
a patient's story or symptoms, I know he or she is suffering from

food sensitivities, and stool tests confirm it. I work by listening to people and tuning in to their energy. Often the blind develop their other senses more keenly; some play a musical instrument exquisitely because they hear things more sharply. Autistic children have a special intuitive sense and presence, but often cannot articulate what they see or feel. I believe that what I have is a gift. My disease has been my teacher, and I suffered long and hard to discover the jewel within.

During my illness, I turned to faith, as many of us do in difficult times."Help me, so I may continue to help others" was my prayer. I repeated it like a mantra, and eventually my prayer was answered. During recent years, it has been amazing to be able to exercise, go for bike rides and hikes, do yoga, or work all day with all the energy and strength I need. My mind is sharper and my thoughts clearer. There is so much to do, and I can now do so much of it! I'd rather be outside, celebrating my new lease on life, than sitting in front of a laptop, but it would be unfair to have this knowledge and not share it. There are so many people still suffering in silence. Some of them find my office. My intention is to reach the rest of them with this book so that they too will find their way back to health. I feel that I was called to write this book, serving as a liaison between the wordy, scientific medical world and those who need to hear this message (anyone who eats food in America). I hope to awaken people from this sleeping epidemic.

I wish you a lifetime of health and blessings in a wonderful world without wheat. Say goodbye to gluten, and hello to a healthy new life, after bread.

CHAPTER 9
Gluten-free Recipes

There are many delicious gluten-free recipes out there. A few of my favorites are included here. Cooking gluten-free foods will show us how to love the foods that are supporting our health and well-being. I recommend stocking your kitchen with a few gluten-free cookbooks. Here are some great ones:

The Gluten-Free Gourmet, Bette Hagman

The Gluten-Free Kitchen, Roben Ryberg

Gluten-Free Quick & Easy, Carol Fenster, Ph.D.

Wheat-Free Recipes & Menus, Carol Fenster, Ph.D.

The Everything Gluten-Free Cookbook, Nancy Maar and Rick Marx

The Best Gluten-Free Family Cookbook, Donna Washburn and Heather Butt

Main Course Recipes

Gluten-free Meatloaf or Turkey Loaf

1½ pounds ground beef or ground turkey
2 eggs
¼ cup cooked brown rice
¼ cup milk (cow, rice, or almond)
2 slices rice bread, crumbled
Pinch of rosemary, oregano, salt

Chop:

1 small onion
2 cloves garlic
2 small tomatoes (or ¼ cup sun-dried tomatoes)
2 celery stalks
2 carrots
Optional: 3 tsp. chopped parsley
¼ cup chopped walnuts

Preheat oven to 375° (all oven temperatures are Fahrenheit).

In a large skillet add oil and sauté the garlic and onions over medium-low heat. Add carrots, celery, and tomatoes. Stir over heat for 10 minutes.

In a bowl combine ground meat, eggs, milk, cooked rice and breadcrumbs. Add salt and seasonings.

This step is best done with clean hands. Mix the sautéed vegetables from the skillet into the bowl. Add parsley and nut, and knead the mixture until combined.

Transfer entire mixture to loaf pan. Bake for 1 hour at 375°

Stir-fried Vegetables and Rice

2 cups of brown rice
1 egg
2 tbs. olive oil (or peanut oil)
2 carrots, diced
1 celery stalk, chopped
½ cup peas
½ cup broccoli (chopped very small)
2 tbs. sesame oil
1 tsp. fresh ginger, diced
1 tsp. fresh garlic, diced
½ cup onion, chopped

Cook brown rice as directed. Prepare vegetables. Heat skillet with oil of choice. Add garlic, ginger, and onion, and stir for 5 minutes. Then add the celery, carrots, peas, and broccoli. When the vegetables become soft, stir in the rice. Beat egg in a bowl. Make a hole in the middle of the rice mixture and add beaten egg. As the egg cooks, mix it in with the rice. Cook until egg is done.

Enjoy this rice with a piece of fresh salmon or chicken.

Salmon Roll Sushi

2 cups cooked brown rice (short grain)
4 sheets sushi nori
1 avocado, sliced
4 oz. smoked salmon
4 green onions
2 tsp. gomasio

For each roll

Lay out one sheet of nori. Spread ½ cup rice on lower half of the sheet.

Place one green onion lengthwise in the center of the roll.

Layer slices of avocado and salmon lengthwise; sprinkle with ½ tsp. of gomasio.

Roll up into a cylinder and cut in half. Makes four rolls.

Quinoa Salad with Asparagus

Quinoa contains all nine essential amino acids, is full of nutrients, and has the highest protein content of any grain. Cooking quinoa is similar to cooking rice, but takes less time.

½ cup quinoa
¼ cup yellow or red bell pepper, chopped
¼ red onion, diced
4 asparagus spears, chopped
1 zucchini, diced
2 mint leaves, minced

Dressing
3 tbs. olive oil
3 tbs. lemon juice
Salt and pepper to taste

Rinse and cook quinoa. Using 1 cup water to ½ cup quinoa, cook over low heat for about 15 minutes. In a skillet, heat oil over medium heat and sauté zucchini, onion, bell pepper, and asparagus until tender (4 minutes). Cool and mix with quinoa. Add mint leaves.

Dressing

Whisk olive oil, lemon salt and pepper. Mix into salad.

Simple Lemon-Pepper Turkey

  1 pound ground white-meat turkey
  2 tbs. butter
  2 tbs. olive oil
  1 cup frozen peas
  Lemon-pepper seasoning (to taste)
  1–2 cups cooked brown rice

Heat butter and olive oil in pan. Sauté turkey until brown. Combine with lemon-pepper seasoning and frozen peas.

Add the brown rice, stir together, and serve.

Chicken Parmesan

  4 boneless and skinless chicken breasts
  2 eggs
  1 cup rice flour (or gluten-free flour)
  1–2 cups rice bread crumbs
  3 tbs. olive oil
  Small jar tomato sauce
  Grated cheese (Parmesan, mozzarella or rice cheese)

Preheat oven to 375°. Heat oil in a large skillet over medium heat.

Using three separate bowls, place rice flour in the first bowl, beat the eggs in the second, and put rice breadcrumbs in the third. Fully coat the chicken breasts one at a time by rolling first in the flour, then in the egg, and finally in the breadcrumbs.

Place all four coated chicken breasts in a heated skillet and brown over medium heat for about 5 minutes. Turn once and brown the other side (add more oil if needed). Place the browned chicken in a baking pan. Top with tomato sauce (about 2–3 tbs. per piece) and grated cheese as desired.

Bake for 30 minutes (longer for larger chicken breasts).

Gluten-free Lasagna (can be made dairy free)

½ cup chopped onion

1 (or more) garlic clove, minced

3½ cups tomato sauce (homemade or jar; with or without meat)

¾ cup water

10 oz. gluten-free lasagna noodles

2 cups ricotta cheese blended with ⅓ cup parmesan cheese (or tofu blend, see below)

1 tablespoon chopped parsley

3 cups chopped vegetables (spinach, green beans, bell peppers, or whatever is in season)

½ cup of pine nuts, lightly browned in a skillet (optional)

Optional: 2 cups shredded mozzarella cheese

Preheat oven to 375°. In a 10-inch skillet, sauté the onion and garlic until soft. Stir in tomato sauce and water. Blend ricotta-parmesan cheese (or tofu blend) and parsley in a food processor. In a 13 x 9-inch baking dish, layer one third of the sauce, half of the uncooked lasagna noodles, half of the ricotta or tofu blend (spread evenly on the uncooked noodles), one half of the chopped vegetables, (and one half of the mozzarella cheese).

Repeat the layers, ending with sauce mixture and pine nuts on top. Cover tightly with foil. Bake one hour. Uncover and let stand for 10 minutes before serving.

This is good with or without the cheese products.

Tofu Blend (the dairy-free option)

24 oz. firm tofu
3 tbs. brewer's yeast
1 teaspoon onion powder
½ teaspoon garlic powder
¾ teaspoon salt
¼ teaspoon dry mustard

Place all ingredients in a food processor and blend till smooth. Spread on the uncooked lasagna noodles as directed.

Gluten-free Homemade French Fries

Potatoes are gluten-free, though eating French fries from restaurants may not be safe since they are often deep-fried in the same oil as other breaded items and may be contaminated with wheat. Here's a simple way to make your own risk-free French fries.

4–6 medium red potatoes
3 tbs. olive oil
Rosemary
Oregano
Salt and pepper

Preheat oven to 375°. Wash the potatoes and cut them into thin slices. Place the potato slices in baking pan and coat with olive oil, salt, and rosemary. Bake for 30 minutes at 375° or to desired crispiness.

Desserts

Gluten-free Piecrust

A simple piecrust, great for pumpkin, squash, or open-top pies.

1 cup rice flour
½ cup almond flour
¼ cup agave nectar or honey
3 tbs. water
3 tbs. oil
½ tsp. cinnamon
Pinch of cloves

In a 9-inch pie plate, combine the almond flour, rice flour, cinnamon, and cloves, mixing these dry ingredients with a fork. Combine the wet ingredients in a bowl, then drizzle over dry mixture and stir with fork until dry ingredients absorb the liquid. This crust will not roll out; shape it in the pie dish by pressing firmly with your fingers. Bake crust for 5 minutes at 350°. Remove from oven, add filling, and bake. Makes one piecrust.

Pumpkin or Squash Pie Filling

¼ cup agave nectar or brown sugar
¼ cup maple syrup
1 tsp. ground ginger
1 tsp cinnamon
½ tsp. salt
1–2 cups fresh pumpkin or butternut squash
2 eggs, beaten

1 cup hot milk (cow, rice, or almond)
Optional: 1 tsp. vanilla

Cut pumpkin or squash into small pieces, and remove all seeds, pulp, and skin.

Place pumpkin (or squash) pieces in a large saucepan with enough water to cover.

Cook on medium-low heat until very soft. Stir frequently, and add more water if needed.

Drain excess water, and let the pumpkin (or squash) cool for one hour.

In a large bowl, mash pumpkin (or squash) well. Blend in maple syrup, agave, and/or sugar. Combine spices, vanilla, and salt. Add the beaten eggs, and mix well. Finally, add hot milk and mix.

Pour into gluten-free pie crust. Bake in preheated oven at 425° for 15 minutes. Reduce heat to 350° and bake another 30 minutes. Filling is done when a fork placed into center of pie comes out clean. Makes one large and delicious pie!

Eydi's Favorite Gluten-free, Dairy-free Chocolate Milk

In a blender combine:

2 cups almond milk
2 tsp. agave nectar

1 tsp. raw cocoa powder
Optional: banana and ice

Blend for 30 seconds and drink.

Chocolate Cake

1½ cups gluten-free flour mix
1 tsp. xanthan gum
2 tbs. cocoa powder
1 tsp. baking powder
1 tsp. baking soda
½ cup maple syrup
2 tbs. molasses
2 eggs
½ cup vegetable oil
½ cup milk (almond, cow, or soy)

Preheat oven to 325°. Grease two 8-inch round cake pans or line them with parchment paper.

Combine the dry ingredients in a large bowl. Add the wet ingredients, and stir for 2 minutes until well blended.

Pour the batter into the two pans, dividing evenly. Bake for 35–45 minutes. Cake is done when a fork inserted in the center comes out clean. Cool for 10 minutes, then turn out onto a wire rack.

Resources and Gluten-free Products

American Celiac Society Dietary Support Coalition
PO Box 23455
New Orleans, LA 70183
www.americanceliacsociety.org

Canadian Celiac Association
5170 Dixie Road, Suite 204
Mississauga, ON L4W 1E3
800-363-7296
www.celiac.ca

Celiac Disease Foundation
13251 Ventura Blvd.
Studio City, CA 91604
818 990-2354
www.celiac.org

Diabetes, Celiac and Me
www.houston.celiacs.org

Enterolab
Testing, Testimonials, and Research www.enterolab.com

Gluten-Free Living
A national magazine dedicated to gluten-free diets
www.glutenfreeliving.com

Gluten Intolerance Group
15110 10th Ave. SW, Suite A
Seattle, Washington 98166
206 246-6652
www.gluten.net

Raising Our Celiac Kids (R.O.C.K.)
3527 Fortuna Ranch Road
Encinitas, CA 92024
www.celiackids.com

www.celiac.com, Celiac.com

Gluten-free Products

Bob's Red Mill
800-553-2258
www.bobsredmill.com
A source of gluten-free cereals

glutenfreeda.com
360-378-3675

Gluten-Free Essentials
877-432-8595
www.gfessentials.com

The Gluten-Free Mall
www.glutenfreemall.com

Gluten-Free Oats
578 Lane 9
Powell, WY 82435
www.glutenfreeoats.com

The Gluten-Free Pantry
800-291-8386
www.glutenfreepantry.com

Glutino
800-363-DIET (3438)
www.glutino.com

Kinnikinnick Foods, Inc.
877-503-4466
www.kinnikinnnick.com

Mary's Gone Crackers
888-258-1250
www.marysgonecrackers.com

Namaste Foods
866-258-9493
www.namastefoods.com

Pamela's Products
200 Clara Ave. Ukiah, CA 95482
707 462-6605
www.pamelasproducts.com

Whole Foods Market
www.wholefoodsmarket.com
Supermarket chain offering gluten-free baked goods

Bibliography

American Diabetes Association

American Journal of Psychiatry. March 2006.

Appleton, Nancy. *Lick the Sugar Habit*. Avery, 1996.

Case, Shelley, B.Sc., RD. *Gluten-Free Diet, A Comprehensive Resource Book*. Dallas, Texas: Helm Publishing, 2006.

Celiac Disease Foundation www.celiac.org

www.Celiac.com

Ford, Rodney, M.D. *Full of it! The shocking truth about gluten*. New Zealand. RRS Global Ltd., 2006.

Golan, Ralph, M.D. *Optimal Wellness: Where Mainstream and Alternative Medicine Meet*. NY: Wellspring/Ballantine, 1995.

Gray, John, Ph. D. *The Mars & Venus Diet & Exercise Solution*. NY: St. Martin's Press, 2003.

Green, Peter H., M.D. *Celiac Disease: A Hidden Epidemic*. NY: HarperCollins Publishers, 2006.

Enterolab: www.enterolab.com

A Personal Touch on Celiac Disease. People Touched by Celiac Disease Sharing Stories to Help You. A Personal Touch Publishing, LLC, 2004.

USA Today headline, Nov. 2006.

Lowell, Jax Peters. *The Gluten-Free Bible: The Thoroughly Indispensable Guide to Negotiating Life Without Wheat.* NY: Henry Holt and Company, LLC, 2005.

Mercola, Dr. Joseph: www.mercola.com

Ross, Harvey, M.D. *Hypoglycemia: The Classic Healthcare Handbook.* NY: Kensington Books, 1996.

Sears, Barry, Ph. D. *The Anti-Inflammation Zone: Reversing the Silent Epidemic That's Destroying Our Health.* NY: HarperCollins Publishers, 2005.

Sears, Barry, Ph.D. *Enter the Zone.* NY: HarperCollins Publishers, 1995.

Time magazine cover, The Secret Killer, the surprising link between inflammation and heart attacks, cancer, Alzheimer's and other diseases. Feb. 2004.

Voelker, R. "Celiac Disease in the United States," JAMA, *The Journal of the American Medical Association*, 2000,283(8):994

Zimmet, P., K. G. Alberti, J. Shaw. "Global and Societal Implications of the Diabetic Epidemic." *Nature*, 2001, 414:782–87.

About the Author

Dr. Eydi Bauer is a chiropractor and applied kinesiologist specializing in clinical nutrition. In 1995 she graduated summa cum laude from Life Chiropractic College-West, with an award for excellence in clinical care, and has been in practice for twelve years. After a many-year battle with undiagnosed celiac disease, she has reclaimed her life and health and has become dedicated to helping others get well by identifying and supporting patients with gluten-related disorders. Dr. Bauer was the director of chiropractic services at the Redwoods Rural Health Center in northern California. She has taught seminars at California's Heartwood Institute and the Omega Institute in New York, and currently teaches private workshops. She now has a private practice in Mendocino, California, where she resides with her eighteen-year-old dog, Chopper, who is also gluten free.